GAY CARD

LIBRETTO

Music by RYAN KORELL

Book & Lyrics by JONATHAN KEEBLER

LICENSING & PRODUCTION INQUIRIES
Uproar Theatrics, LLC.
hello@uproartheatrics.com I www.UproarTheatrics.com

Gay Card
Music copyright © 2016 by Ryan Korell
Book and Lyrics copyright © 2016 by Jonathan Keebler

Gay Card is published by Uproar Theatrics, LLC
500 8th Ave FRNT 3, #1714 New York, NY 10018

ISBN: 978-1-968051-20-4

First Printing, May 2025

CAST OF CHARACTERS

LOGAN: Male. 18. Enthusiastic, awkward, and obsessive. He desperately wants to shed his loser skin and have an awesome college life full of friends, fun, and love.

MELANIE: Female. 18. Logan's best friend since middle school. Logical, direct, yet warm over-achiever. She never wants to be perceived as immature.

GRAHAM: Male. 18. Logan's eventual love interest. Opinionated, easy-presence, but a bit of a chip on his shoulder. He likes to be looked up to.

DANIELLE: Female. 21. R.A. of Diversity House. A snarky, tell-it-like-it-is diva who loves to party and hates to let people see beyond

JUSTIN: Female. 21. R.A. of Diversity House. A snarky, tell-it-like-it-is diva who loves to party and hates to let people see beyond

JULY: Female. 18. A lesbian who practices new age spirituality.

CORY: Male. 18. An intensely sexual bisexual guy.

BLOG TRIO/ENSEMBLE: 2 Male, 1 Female. 18-22. Blog: The personification of the Gay Card Blog, a guide to being gay in college written by someone who has mastered it. Like any blog, it wants to be followed. Also plays: High Schoolers, College Students, Club Guys, Art Fags, Gay-mers, A Ca-Homos, Gay Bros, Pride Paraders, Rodrick Richards, and Partiers.

ADDITIONAL ENSEMBLE: Optional. 18-22. Any number/genders. Additional ensemble members may play High Schoolers, College Students, Club Guys, Art Fags, Gay-mers, A Ca-Homos, Gay Bros, Pride Paraders, and Partiers.

SETTING

PLACE: In and around Lakeshore College in central Florida

TIME: 2010

SCENE / MUSIC BREAKDOWN

ACT 1

I-1. HIGHSCHOOL / AROUND LAKESHORE CAMPUS
1.   PROLOGUE
Instrumental
2.   STARTING NOW
Logan, Melanie, Company

I-2. DIVERSITY HOUSE COMMON ROOM
3.   WHAT IT FEELS LIKE TO BELONG
Logan

I-3. COMPUTER LAB
4.   FOLLOW ME
Blog Trio, Logan

I-4. COMMON ROOM / PORTAL, A GAY CLUB
5.   FAKE ID
Danielle, Company
6.   FAKE ID II / LOOK AT ME
Graham, Company

I-5. PORTAL PARKING LOT
7.   ALL FIGURED OUT
Melanie

I-6. AROUND LAKESHORE CAMPUS
8.   BETTER
Logan, Company

I-7. THE LAKE
9.   STEP BACK
Graham, Logan
9A. WEEKS GO BY / STEP BACK (REPRISE)
Instrumental, Graham, Logan

I-8. COMMON ROOM / PRIDE PARADE
9B. HEY THERE, MELANIE
Justin
10. PERFECT DAY
Company
11. EVERYBODY ELSE / PERFECT DAY II
Melanie, Logan, Graham, Company

ACT II

ACT I

SCENE ONE

> *(Darkness. SPOT ON LOGAN, center stage, opening a laptop that sits on a desk in front of him. He addresses the audience)*

LOGAN
Hello, internet, and welcome to my new channel. I'm Logan Kappler.

> *(He holds up a card with handwritten scribbles on it)*

LOGAN
This is my Gay Card. I know it doesn't look like much, but this is proof of my identity. Back at the start of my freshman year, I thought getting this thing, being the guy I am, was as easy as saying "I'm gay." Boy, was I wrong.

2. STARTING NOW... LOGAN, MELANIE, COMPANY

> *(LIGHTS OUT. Logan's video blog narration is taken over by a recorded voiceover of him narrating. The actor is no longer speaking this narration)*

LOGAN
(Voiceover)
We're starting off with high school me, packing up to go to Lakeshore College, Central Florida. I was ready to leave my

1

tiny little town of Kowachobee behind. And I was so sure the
hard part was over.

> *(LIGHTS UP. LOGAN is packing a suitcase. He
> is now wearing a baggy t-shirt, baggy shorts,
> and bulky sneakers, all in hideously matched
> neutral colors. And his hair is a disaster)*

LOGAN
SAY GOODBYE TO MY HIGH SCHOOL LIFE
AND ITS WEIRD UNWRITTEN RULES.
SAY GOODBYE TO MY HIGH SCHOOL PEERS
WHO WERE ALL SUCH TOTAL TOOLS.
SAY HELLO TO PEOPLE WHO GET ME,
WHO SEE THINGS MORE MY WAY.
ONCE I'M ON THAT COLLEGE CAMPUS,
I KNOW JUST WHAT I'LL SAY:

EV'RY STEP'S A STEP ON MY OWN,
HERE I AM CLEARING THE SLATE.
I'M ERASING ALL THAT I'VE KNOWN,
AND STARTING NOW, LIFE'S GREAT.

LOGAN
(Voiceover)
I didn't have many friends in high school. But senior year,
when I realized I was gay, I knew that things were gonna
change. If the internet taught me anything, it was that gay
people are *awesome*. Therefore, I was going to be awesome!
Unfortunately, my peers didn't quite agree.

> *(Memories of HIGH SCHOOLERS interrupt
> LOGAN'S packing)*

HIGH SCHOOL DUDE
WAIT, YOU'RE GAY?

HIGH SCHOOL GAY
BUT I'VE HEARD YOU SAY
YOU'VE NEVER ONCE HEARD GAGA SING!

HIGH SCHOOL CHICK
NO WAY!

HIGH SCHOOL DUDE
YOU DON'T WEAR PINK.

HIGH SCHOOL CHICK
YOU KNOW WHAT I THINK?
THIS IS AN ATTENTION THING.

(The HIGHSCHOOLERS DISAPPEAR)

LOGAN
BUT SOON I'LL BE IN A LIFE OF MY CHOOSING,
AND NOT ONE THAT CHOSE ME.
AND ONCE I'M WITH MY COLLEGE BUDDIES,
I KNOW THEY'LL ALL AGREE:

*(SPOT ON college students JUSTIN, JULY,
CORY, and DANIELLE who have appeared with
suitcases upstage)*

LOGAN, JUSTIN, JULY, CORY, DANIELLE
EV'RY STEP'S A STEP ON MY OWN,
HERE I AM CLEARING THE SLATE.
I'M ERASING ALL THAT I'VE KNOWN,
AND STARTING NOW, LIFE'S GREAT.

LOGAN
(Voiceover)
I was packed and ready to go! Unfortunately, I still had three months of summer left. Did I mention I tend to rush into things without thinking?

HIGH SCHOOL GAY
I'm going to join Lakeshore College's LGBTQQIAA club.

LOGAN
Summer was never ending. There was one gay guy in Kowachobee and we didn't click.

HIGH SCHOOL GAY
THEY'RE GONNA LOVE ME IN THIS CLUB.

LOGAN
YOU'RE GONNA JOIN? I MIGHT JUST DO THE SAME.

HIGH SCHOOL GAY
WELL, BEING GAY'S *MY* THING,
BUT "ALLY" IS IN THE NAME.

LOGAN
COME ON, YOU KNOW I'M ALSO GAY,
I TOLD YOU LAST WEEK AND THE WEEK
BEFORE –

HIGH SCHOOL GAY
BUT, LOGAN, IF YOU'RE GAY,
IT ISN'T COOL ANYMORE.

LOGAN
(Voiceover)
Who needed some dumb LG-whatever club, Lakeshore had
something even better: a freshman dorm called Diversity
House.

LOGAN
THEY'RE GONNA LOVE ME IN THIS HOUSE,
HISPANIC, GAY, OR JEW, IT'S ALL OKAY.
"INCLUSIVE" IS IN THEIR CREED!

HIGH SCHOOL DUDE
Wow, dude, that really sounds gay.

LOGAN
Glad you finally see it.

HIGH SCHOOL DUDE
MY BAD, BY GAY I MORE MEANT LAME,
REAL GAYS ARE AWESOME AND MORE COOL
THAN YOU.

LOGAN
MY NEW FRIENDS WON'T AGREE.

HIGH SCHOOL CHICK
BUT, LOGAN, WHAT IF THEY DO?

LOGAN
(Voiceover)
Of course, there was no way that was stopping me from
applying.

*(LOGAN fills out the Diversity House
application)*

5

LOGAN
SAY GOODBYE TO THOSE HIGH SCHOOL KIDS
AND THEIR STUPID HIGH SCHOOL JOKES.
SAY GOODBYE TO THE TEENAGE MINDS
IN THOSE SMALL-TOWN HIGH SCHOOL FOLKS.
SAY HELLO TO WHAT I KNOW I'LL FIND IN
THAT MORE INVITING PLACE –
OF COURSE, I COULD DO WITH SOME BACKUP,
I MEAN, WELL, JUST IN CASE…

*(MELANIE ENTERS with two cups of frozen
yogurt and hands one to LOGAN)*

MELANIE
All right, last day in Kowachobee. I made a checklist!

LOGAN
(Voiceover)
That's Melanie, my best friend since middle school.

MELANIE
Final fro-yo, check; finish packing, check; load the truck,
check; get gas, check –

LOGAN
Say yes to living in Diversity House?
(LOGAN hands her a letter)
I sent in an application for you.

MELANIE
This is about the gay thing again, isn't it?

LOGAN
Maybe.

MELANIE

If I'm gonna get my mathematics degree in three years, I can't be filling up my schedule with extraneous social activities.

LOGAN

Please. I need you. Yearbook pictures, SAT prep, AP Calc – I only got through all that with your help.

MELANIE

You *are* systematically hopeless.

LOGAN

Exactly. I'll even throw in a fro-yo date every Friday night for good measure.

MELANIE

Well, that's a given. So, you want me to help you be gay in college?

LOGAN

I want us to have an awesome college experience – together.
(He grabs her hand)
THERE FOR EACH OTHER.
WE'VE ALWAYS BEEN THERE FOR EACH OTHER.

LOGAN, MELANIE

WHEN OTHERS LOG OFF AND SIGN OUT,
NO DOUBT, YOU'VE BEEN MY GUARANTEE.

LOGAN

WHEN YOU'RE WITH ME, I'VE GOT NOTHING TO FEAR,
COME ON, LET'S MAKE AN INCREDIBLE YEAR,
THE PAST IS THE PAST, THE FUTURE IS HERE,
JUST THINK OF WHAT THAT COULD BE.

MELANIE
(Giving in)
THERE FOR EACH OTHER.

LOGAN

Yes!

MELANIE
WE'LL ALWAYS BE THERE FOR EACH OTHER.

LOGAN, MELANIE
THAT'S WHAT IS CONSTANT, YOU AND I.
AS FOR OUR PAST, SAY GOODBYE.

*(THEY grab two suitcases as STUDENTS
ENTER. It's the first day of freshman year!)*

MELANIE
SAY GOODBYE TO OUR HIGH SCHOOL TOWN
AND ITS CRASS MORONIC SPELL!

LOGAN
SAY GOODBYE TO OUR HIGH SCHOOL LIVES
NOTHING ELSE COULD MATCH THAT HELL!

CORY
SAY GOODBYE TO MY HIGH SCHOOL FRIENDS
SOMETIMES PEOPLE GROW APART.

JULY
SAY GOODBYE TO MY HIGH SCHOOL SELF,
TIME TO LET THIS NEW LIFE START!

ALL
SAY HELLO, FOR COLLEGE IS WAITING
MUST GET IN ITS GROOVE.
I MIGHT SEEM ANCHORED TO MY PAST,
BUT BY MAY I SWEAR I'LL PROVE

EV'RY STEP'S A STEP ON MY OWN,
HERE I AM CLEARING THE SLATE.
I'M ERASING ALL THAT I'VE KNOWN,
I'M EMBRACING HOW I HAVE GROWN,

LOGAN
(Voiceover)
I was ready to be myself for the first time in my life! Did I
do it? You tell me.

WOMEN	**MEN**	**LOGAN**
STARTING	STARTING	
NOW…	NOW…	SAY HELLO TO
STARTING	STARTING	MY BRAND-
NOW…	NOW…	NEW LIFE
YES, I KNOW	STARTING	WITH SO
	NOW…	MANY NEW
		THINGS THAT I
IN MY HEART	NOT SURE	CAN DO:
	HOW,	BUY A BOOK,
STARTING	BUT I VOW	LEARN TO
NOW –	STARTING	COOK,
	NOW –	TRY A DRINK,
		TEXT A WINK,
		TAKE A PIC,
		FIND A CLIQUE,
		STARTING
		NOW –

(THEY arrive at Diversity House. DANIELLE is waiting)

DANIELLE
Welcome to Diversity House!

ALL
LIFE'S GREAT!

END OF SCENE

SCENE TWO

(Common Room of Diversity House.

*LOGAN, MELANIE, and three other
DIVERSITY HOUSE MEMBERS, JUSTIN,
JULY and CORY, are listening to DANIELLE)*

DANIELLE

Okay, so the R.A. manual says I have to say this: you are
living in Diversity House, a living learning community at
Lakeshore College devoted to understanding and celebrating
diversity on our multicultural, future-focused campus, blah,
blah, blah. Get it? Okay, let's sign some forms. July.

JULY

Right here.

DANIELLE

What kind of name is July?

JULY

My mom named me April. Do I look like an April?

(JULY CROSSES to fill out her forms)

CORY
(To Melanie)

I'm Cory. You're cute.

MELANIE

Me?

CORY

We should hook up later. I'd love to have you as my college first.

MELANIE

Oh.

DANIELLE

Melanie.

MELANIE

Woops. Darn, my name.

(MELANIE CROSSES AWAY. JULY RETURNS)

JUSTIN

Living in Diversity House, you guys psyched for this or what?

JULY

So, did you find out yet?

LOGAN

Find out what?

DANIELLE

Cory.

(CORY CROSSES AWAY. MELANIE RETURNS)

CORY
(To July)

They're all yours.

JULY

Cory and I have been playing "guess the diversity."

LOGAN

That's awesome! Well, I'm – !

JULY

That's not how it works. Okay, let's see:
(She does a magical motion of her hands to Melanie)
Mmm…lll…Lesbian.
(The same to Logan)
And… tough one… Scientologist?

LOGAN

Not even close, I'm –

DANIELLE

Logan.

LOGAN

Bah! Okay, be right back. I know, the suspense is killing you.
(LOGAN CROSSES AWAY. CORY RETURNS)

CORY

Conclusions?

JULY

Scientologist, lesbian –

CORY

Lesbian, that explains it.

MELANIE

I'm not a lesbian.

JULY

That's too bad.

CORY

Then why are you here?

MELANIE

I'm here for Logan. You see he's –

(LOGAN RETURNS)

LOGAN

Okay. So you were totally wrong about me being a
Scientologist –

DANIELLE

Justin.

JUSTIN

Yo.

(JUSTIN CROSSES to DANIELLE)

CORY

What do you think *his* thing is? Jewish?

JULY

No, they only come to Florida to retire.

DANIELLE

Stop by my room later if you need any – mentoring.

(DANIELLE SLAPS JUSTIN'S butt)

MELANIE

That seemed inappropriate.

(JUSTIN returns to the group)

JUSTIN
Talk about a sexually charged house, right?

MELANIE
I don't really do sex – I mean I don't do relationships – I mean I don't engage in any sort of –

LOGAN
You know, speaking of sexuality –

DANIELLE
Graham. Graham, anybody?

(GRAHAM ENTERS hurriedly)

GRAHAM
Sorry. Sorry. I'm here.

DANIELLE
You're late.

GRAHAM
My flight was delayed. It was a rough start.

CORY
Looks like someone needs to be soothed. I give great back rubs.

MELANIE
Weren't you hitting on me a minute ago?

CORY
I'm bisexual. I'm attracted to beauty and passion. I don't discriminate.

LOGAN

You're bi? I'm –

JUSTIN

Bisexual people, that's so cool. Are you bi, Graham?

GRAHAM

Oh wow, we're making that the first question? If you gotta know, I'm gay, but –

LOGAN

I'm gay too!!!

(Long awkward silence)

DANIELLE

Soo… Graham, sign your papers?

(GRAHAM CROSSES to do so)

LOGAN

Did you guys hear me? I'm gay.

JULY

That's… that's nice?

LOGAN

We saw all these shirtless swimmer guys on the way here. Dreamboats. I'm sure they're straight, but –

CORY

Sorry, but you don't seem gay.

MELANIE

I know he can come off that way, the old clothes, the sad hair, the desperate puppy dog thing – I totally thought he was straight for years, but –

LOGAN

Not helping.

(Beat)

Do I come off as straight or something?

JUSTIN

Dude, no.

DANIELLE

Freshman, it's not about being straight. Gay people are awesome.

LOGAN

Right, therefore I am awesome.

DANIELLE

Therefore, you don't seem gay. Not twink-y gay, not bro-y gay, not nerd-y gay. Not gay.

CORY

Gay Card revoked! Am I right, guys?

JUSTIN

Wait, what's a Gay Card?

GRAHAM

It's supposed to be, like, the proof that you're a quote-unquote "true gay." It's really narrow-minded.

JUSTIN

And he took that away? Can he do that?

CORY

Are we done with check-in?

DANIELLE

Yeah, yeah. Go party it up. Justin, how about that "mentoring?"

JUSTIN

Well... I do want to learn as much about diversity as possible.

DANIELLE

That's so cute.

(DANIELLE and JUSTIN EXIT)

CORY

July, Graham, movie night in my room? I have a leopard print couch, it's so soft. Melanie, you're welcome to join us.

LOGAN

I'm totally in!

CORY

The room's kinda small. Four's pretty much the limit. Movie starts in ten, kittens.

(CORY, JULY, and GRAHAM EXIT)

MELANIE

You'll get 'em next time.

LOGAN
(Distracted)

Next time.

MELANIE

We should go get fro-yo, celebrate our first night at college.

LOGAN

I'm not in the mood for fro-yo.

(LOGAN COLLAPSES ON THE COUCH and pulls out his phone)

MELANIE

Logan, they were just kidding around, you shouldn't –

LOGAN

Look, you better get going. Don't want to miss the start of the movie.

MELANIE

What does it matter if people don't think you're gay? It's your sexuality; it's kind of personal anyway. It doesn't define you.

3. WHAT IT FEELS LIKE TO BELONG............ LOGAN

LOGAN

Come here.

(MELANIE SITS, LOGAN shows her his phone)

MELANIE

It's Donald Sutters' Facebook page, so what?
(LOGAN taps the phone)
And Richie Walters'.
(Another tap)
And Eric McConnell's; where are you going with this?

LOGAN
ALL THROUGHOUT HIGH SCHOOL,
I SAT IN MY BEDROOM
WISHING TO BE SOMEONE ELSE.

MELANIE
Okay.

LOGAN
SWIPING AND SCROLLING,
AND STARING AT PICTURES,
AND WISHING TO BE SOMEONE ELSE.
BUT THIS WAS MY CHANCE HERE,
THE THING THAT WOULD CHANGE THINGS,
AND SAVE ME FROM WHO I WAS THEN.
YET HERE I AM SITTING,
AND STARING AT PICTURES,
AND WISHING TO BE SOMEONE ELSE AGAIN.

HERE'S A PICTURE
OF A PERSON
THAT WE KNEW FROM OUR HOMETOWN.
IT'S HIS FIRST NIGHT
AT A NEW SCHOOL
AND A WHOLE LOT'S GOING DOWN.
HE TRIES A SHOT OF SMIRNOFF,
STRIKES A POSE,
THEN SOMEONE CHATS HIS EAR OFF,
AND NO ONE KNOWS
BACK IN HIGH SCHOOL
HE WAS NOTHING –
NOW A NEW LIFE'S COME ALONG,
AND THE WAY HE'S SMILING SHOWS
WHAT IT FEELS LIKE TO BELONG.

LOGAN (CONT)

EV'RY PICTURE
THAT I LOOK AT
IS A STORY MUCH LIKE HIS.
PEOPLE FINDING
NEW BEGINNINGS,
UNDETERRED BY HOW LIFE IS.
ONE'S POSING LIKE A MODEL,
SO CAREFREE!
ONE'S PLAYING SPIN THE BOTTLE –
WHY NOT ME?
THEY ALL FIT IN
WHAT'S THEIR SECRET?
TELL ME, WHERE HAVE I GONE WRONG?
WILL I EVER GET TO SEE
WHAT IT FEELS LIKE TO BELONG?

THIS IS THE GUY WHO'S GONE HIS WHOLE LIFE
ALWAYS FEELING PUSHED OFF TO THE SIDE.
THIS IS THE GUY WHO'D GIVE ALL HE'S GOT
TO FINALLY FEEL HE CAN JOIN IN THE RIDE.
I WANT LOVE! I WANT FRIENDS!
AND A STORY THAT ENDS
WITH ME BIDDING MY OLD SELF GOODBYE
AND CHANGING THE KIND OF GUY I AM

TO A PERSON
IN A PICTURE
WITH A WHOLE CROWD BY HIS SIDE.
WE ARE LAUGHING,
WE ARE DANCING,
AND THE WORLD HAS OPENED WIDE.
AND WITHOUT ANY WARNING
FEELINGS SOAR!

LOGAN (CONT)
I'M STAYING OUT 'TIL MORNING,
AND WHAT'S MORE:
I AM HAPPY,
I AM WANTED,
I AM HANDSOME, BOLD, AND STRONG!
NO MORE CLAWING AT LIFE'S HEELS,
I AM LIVING IN IDEALS,
AND MY SMILING FACE REVEALS
WHAT IT FEELS LIKE TO BELONG!

END OF SCENE

SCENE THREE

(The Computer Lab.

MELANIE is furiously working at a computer. She is the only one there. JUSTIN ENTERS, carrying a cup of coffee)

JUSTIN
(Miming a doorbell)

Ding-dong.

MELANIE

It's a public space, there's no need for a doorbell.

JUSTIN

I think you're the only one who still actually uses the computer lab.
(Hands her the coffee)
Thought you might need a caffeine boost. I've been in the section nearby. Brushing up on my queer literature and stuff like that.

MELANIE

No offense, but I took you for more of a jock: not so into the queer… or the reading.

JUSTIN

You caught me; I'm a secret evil jock attempting to destroy Diversity House from the inside.

MELANIE

I didn't say evil.

JUSTIN

Let's just say I'm trying to expand my horizons.
(Beat)
So, what class is giving you so much work this fast?

MELANIE

It's not for class. I'm doing research for Logan about how to make people believe he's gay.

JUSTIN

You're not serious.

MELANIE

I'm always serious.

JUSTIN

Well, I'm sure this is a totally duh thing, but you've checked this out, right?

(HE types an address on MELANIE'S computer)

MELANIE

Where did you find this?

JUSTIN

I may have done some really in-depth googling to write my entrance essay for Diversity House.

MELANIE

I've been looking for something like this all day!

JUSTIN

It's not like super popular or anything. And it's pretty new. It seems like the writer actually goes to Lakeshore. Crazy right?

MELANIE

It's perfect. I'm texting Logan right now!
(Sends a text)
How can I thank you?

JUSTIN

Well, since we're all going clubbing tonight, save me a
dance or two? Maybe have a drink with me?

MELANIE

If this is some sort of romantic proposition, I have to decline.

JUSTIN

Look, if it's about Danielle, she and I just hooked up a few
times, we're not –

MELANIE

You two are hooking up?

JUSTIN

Foot meet mouth. Guess I'm kinda sucking at defying the
whole jock impression.

MELANIE

It's fine. I don't actually do dating. I have a plan. It's very
thorough, and it doesn't have much room for distractions.

JUSTIN

Except for helping your friend be gay?

MELANIE

Logan tends to be the exception.

(LOGAN ENTERS)

LOGAN

I got your text!

MELANIE

That was fast.

JUSTIN

Well, see you around, Melanie.

MELANIE

Bye, Justin.

(JUSTIN EXITS)

LOGAN

He's totally into you.

MELANIE

Irrelevant. Say thank you.

LOGAN

Thank you. Why am I thanking you?

MELANIE

I've solved all your problems.

> *(SHE hits a button on her computer and A BLOG PAGE DISPLAYS ON A PROJECTION SCREEN NEARBY. It includes three pictures: a skinny gay guy (Blog 1), a muscled gay guy (Blog 2), and a woman who evokes a female gay icon (Blog 3). A huge title overhead reads "Gay Card Blog")*

LOGAN

The "Gay Card Blog?"

MELANIE
(Reading from the Blog)
"A novice homosexual's guide to being gay in college.
Don't have your gay card? Lost your gay card? You've come
to the right anonymous internet personality."

LOGAN
I don't know about this.

4. FOLLOW ME............................ BLOG TRIO, LOGAN

MELANIE
Do you want them to believe you're gay or not? Listen.

*(THE SCREEN RISES. Behind it stands the
BLOG TRIO, manifestations of the three pictures
we saw on the blog page before)*

BLOG TRIO
OOO…

MELANIE
"Getting your gay card means fun!"

BLOG TRIO
OOO…

MELANIE
"Getting your gay card means sex!"

BLOG TRIO
OOO…

MELANIE
"Getting your gay card means you belong!"

BLOG TRIO
OOO!

Subscribe to me, and you'll get it!

MELANIE
I'll give you a chance to read it over.

(MELANIE EXITS)

LOGAN
How is this supposed to help me?

BLOG TRIO
Gay Card Blog Post number 1: I am your fairy blog father.

BLOG 1
YOU'RE FAILING AT BEING GAY.
WOAH, OH.

BLOG 3
YOU WANNA GO HIDE AWAY.
WOAH, OH.

BLOG 2
YOU SAY, WELL, WHAT CAN I DO?
THAT'S THE WAY THINGS ARE.

BLOG 1
BUT LISTEN, I'M TELLING YOU
I CAN GET YOU BACK ON PAR.
I'LL SPELL IT OUT FOR YOU:

BLOG 3
CLICK THAT BUTTON AND FOLLOW ME!

BLOG 2
EV'RY HOTTIE'S GONNA CRAWL AT YOUR FEET.

BLOG 1
I'M YOUR LOG-IN, YOUR PASS, YOUR KEY!

BLOG 2
YOU'LL BE SOMEONE THEY WANNA MEET,

BLOG TRIO
WHEN YOU'RE FOLLOWING ME.

BLOG 1
YEAH.

LOGAN
I already came out. That should be enough.

BLOG TRIO
Bad news: coming out's the easy part.

BLOG 2
Now you've gotta find out which kind of gay guy you are.

BLOG 3
Preferably by the end of your first semester. My data suggests you've only got a 5% chance after that.

LOGAN
I'm doomed.

BLOG 3
IT'S DAUNTING, OH HELL I KNOW.

LOGAN
YEAH, YEAH.

BLOG 2
YOUR FEARS ARE ALL APROPOS.

LOGAN
YEAH, YEAH.

BLOG 1
MOST PEOPLE WOULD HAVE NO SHOT.

LOGAN
I HAVE NO SHOT!

BLOG 1
THEY'D BE RIGHT TO FLEE.

LOGAN
I SHOULD FLEE!

BLOG 2, 3
BUT MOST PEOPLE, MY FRIEND, YOU'RE NOT,

LOGAN
I'M NOT?

BLOG 2, 3
'CAUSE BUDDY, YOU'VE GOT ME!

BLOG 1
SO, I REITERATE:

BLOG TRIO
CLICK THAT BUTTON AND FOLLOW ME!

BLOG 2
YOU'LL BOOK EV'RY NIGHT FROM NOW UNTIL
MAY.

BLOG TRIO
THERE'S NO CHARGE AND NO ADS, I'M FREE!

BLOG 3
LIFE'S A GAME YOU GET TO PLAY,

BLOG TRIO
WHEN YOU'RE FOLLOWING ME.

BLOG 2
LET ME BREAK IT DOWN NOW:
THERE ARE MANY TYPES OF GAY BOYS
AND I SAY, BOY, FIND A TYPE YOU FIT:

BLOG 3
AN AIRY TWINK,

BLOG 1
A KINKY BEAR,

BLOG 2
I PINKY SWEAR –

BLOG TRIO, LOGAN
IT'S OUT THERE!

BLOG 3
I'LL ADVISE YOU, I'LL WISE YOU UP:

BLOG 1
AN OTTER THAT'S HOTTER,
PERHAPS A GAY BRO THAT'S
WAY MO' BRO THAN THE STRAIGHT BRO!

BLOG TRIO, LOGAN
HEY-O!

BLOG 3

I SAY-O!

BLOG 2

THERE'S A MILLION DIFFERENT SCENES FOR
YOU TO DO,

BLOG 1, 2

AND AMONG THEM

BLOG TRIO

YOU WILL FIND A GAY CARD RIGHT FOR YOU!

LOGAN

FOR ME!

BLOG TRIO

SO, CLICK THAT BUTTON AND FOLLOW ME!

LOGAN

I'D FIN'LY FIND A WAY TO BELONG.

BLOG TRIO

DON'T DEBATE IT, JUST CLICK AGREE!

LOGAN

I MEAN, REALLY, I CAN'T GO WRONG.

BLOG TRIO

WHEN YOU'RE FOLLOWING ME.

LOGAN

I'LL FOLLOW YOU!

BLOG TRIO

YEAH!

BLOG TRIO
WHEN YOU'RE FOLLOWING ME!
YEAH!

END OF SCENE

SCENE FOUR

LOGAN
(Voiceover)
My quest for my gay card had begun! I would tell you about
my excursion to the mall that afternoon to buy some new
clothes, but it's honestly just too shameful to talk about.
We'll just skip ahead to that evening.

(Diversity House Common Room.

*CORY and JULY are standing. They are dressed
for clubbing, Cory's outfit particularly risqué.
GRAHAM is on the couch, writing on his phone)*

CORY
How's this for the club?

JULY
Depends. What are you going for?

CORY
Sort of a Rodrick Richards look.

JULY
Who?

CORY
Rodrick Richards. Star of *Life of Rod*? Winner of this year's
Orlando Gay and Lesbian film festival!

GRAHAM
Wasn't that film basically soft-core porn?

CORY

Exactly!

JULY

Ugh. You're like this girl I dated over the summer: a delicate flower on the inside who contorted into a gross, perverted beast on the outside. She was denying her inner spirit! It was a desperate plea for attention.

CORY

Are you calling me desperate?

GRAHAM

You do have the whole greedy bisexual thing going.

CORY

That's an offensive stereotype.

JULY

Very offensive.

(MELANIE ENTERS)

CORY

Melanie, isn't that offensive?

MELANIE

Sorry, what are you guys talking about?

CORY

Graham, I expect you to dress up extra hot for me tonight to make up for your rude comment.

GRAHAM

Please, I wouldn't be caught dead at a gay club.

(GRAHAM EXITS. An ELABORATE KNOCK is heard)

MELANIE

It's time!

CORY

Time for what?

MELANIE
(Poking her head into a room)

You all set?
(Back out)
Members of Diversity House, I'd like to introduce you to the fabulous, new and improved, homo of homos: Logan Kappler.

(LOGAN ENTERS. HE now wears short, neon-colored shorts, a tight tank top, and a pair of large sunglasses)

LOGAN

You ready to party? I am!

(LOGAN attempts to do a dance move featuring his butt – it is less than successful. BLOG NOTIFICATION SOUND. The BLOG TRIO APPEARS)

BLOG 2

Gay Card Blog post number 5: for the novice gay just starting out in his quest for his gay card, perhaps a classic approach is best.

BLOG 1
The Twink, with his youthful look, tight clothing, and skinny physique, just screams classic gay.

BLOG 3
The Twink pairs nicely with a night of clubbing and is highly recommended for any college gay who foresees many nights on the dance floor in his future.

BLOG 2
A word of caution, the Twink is only for a select body type.

BLOG TRIO
Those above super skinny need not apply.

(BLOG TRIO DISAPPEARS)

JULY
What happened to you?

LOGAN
New look. You like?

JULY
It's tight.

LOGAN
Like, cool tight?

CORY
Like, she-hopes-you-have-a-backup-when-it-rips tight.

> *(DANIELLE ENTERS, super done-up, glitter everywhere. JUSTIN ENTERS behind her, carrying a laminator)*

DANIELLE

Okay, everybody here?

(Seeing LOGAN)

Woah. You gotta warn people before they see all that.

(To the group)

Do we got a D.D.? Anyone? Graham! Get out here! You're gonna be designated driver!

(GRAHAM REENTERS)

GRAHAM

And why would I want to drag your butts to some lame gay club –

(Sees Logan)

Did you lose a bet?

LOGAN

I'm a Twink now!

GRAHAM

This I've got to see. Fine, I'll drive.

DANIELLE

Perfect. Alright. Justin, the laminator.

(JUSTIN sets the laminator down)

DANIELLE

Good boy.

LOGAN

What's that for?

DANIELLE

For Fake IDs. You're in luck, freshmen, because not only is
your R.A. hot and fabulous, she also has a talent for forgery.

CORY

You're either the best R.A. ever or the worst R.A. ever, I
can't decide.

LOGAN

But we're 18. We can get into clubs at 18.

DANIELLE

But you can't drink. Believe me, you don't want to be sober
at a club. Alright everyone, pick who you want to be tonight,
and I'll create your new persona.

GRAHAM

Shouldn't we just be ourselves but older?

5. FAKE ID................................. DANIELLE, COMPANY

DANIELLE
YOU THINK IT'S ALL THAT SIMPLE?
YOU THINK THAT *YOU'RE* ENOUGH?
YOU THINK THAT YOU'RE SUCH *HOT* STUFF?
THAT YOU WILL BE IMMORTAL?
YOU THINK YOU'RE UP TO PAR?
THIS AIN'T NO SMALL-TOWN GAY BAR.
THIS IS PORTAL!
THE HOTTEST GAY CLUB IN CENTRAL FLORIDA.

LOOK, YOU'RE ALL FRESHMEN,
HORMONES RACING DEEP INSIDE YOU.
BUT, CLUBS ARE CRAZY,
SO YOU BETTER LET ME GUIDE YOU.

DANIELLE (CONT)
YOU NEED A DRIVER,
PARKING'S A FIVER,
BAGS SHOULD BE SMALL.
HAVE PHONES YOU CAN CLING TO,
MUSIC TO SING TO,
BUT MOST OF ALL

YOU WILL NEED A FAKE ID,
MEMORIZE THIS BRAND-NEW YOU,
AND I PROMISE YOU WILL SEE
LIFE IS GREAT FOR PEOPLE WHO
HAVE A FAKE ID

(Portal, a Gay Club.

Lots of PEOPLE are dancing in the dark and only the occasional flashes of light illuminate them. SPOT ON LOGAN and MELANIE)

LOGAN
My first time at a gay club! The lights, the music, it's beautiful. What do I do now?

MELANIE
Get out there and dance! "Get your groove on," so to speak.

(On the other side of the club, GRAHAM is sipping a drink and typing intently on his phone. CORY APPROACHES HIM)

CORY
Texting my competition?

GRAHAM
Taking notes. People-watching at clubs is priceless.

(CLUB GUY 1 APPROACHES HIM)

CLUB GUY 1
Can I buy you a drink?

GRAHAM
No.

CLUB GUY 1
Guys who don't give a fuck are hot.

GRAHAM
Guys who don't give a fuck are also not interested in you.

> *(LOGAN does a really dorky dance move next to CLUB GUY 2)*

LOGAN
I call this move the Kappler!

CLUB GUY 2
That's embarrassing.

(CLUB GUY 2 CROSSES AWAY from LOGAN)

LOGAN
Maybe dancing's not my thing.

MELANIE
Okay, come here –

LOGAN
What are you doing?

MELANIE
Demonstrating.

*(MELANIE starts dancing around Logan
erotically)*

MELANIE
YOU'VE GOTTA BREAKOUT.
GOTTA SHAKE IT LIKE YOU GOT ONE.

DANIELLE
PUT OUT AN IMAGE,
AND IT BETTER BE A HOT ONE.

CORY
DANCE TO THE GROOVE RIGHT,

JULY
GET EV'RY MOVE RIGHT.

CORY AND JULY
GUYS, GET IN SYNC.

ALL
IF YOUR PERSONA
DRINKS A CORONA,
THAT'S WHAT YOU DRINK.

DON'T YOU LOSE YOUR FAKE ID,
KEEP UP WITH THIS BRAND NEW YOU.
TRUST ME, HONEY, LIFE CAN BE,
BETTER THAN YOU EVER KNEW
WITH YOUR FAKE ID

LOGAN
Who are you and what have you done with my best friend?

MELANIE

That was kind fun, right? Amazing what a little research can do.

DANIELLE

That's right, girl! Looks like the geek has a little freak in her!

LOGAN

You're sure making an impression.

MELANIE

Don't get distracted, eye on the goal. Go!

(MELANIE pushes LOGAN towards CLUB GUY 1. JULY approaches GRAHAM)

JULY

I don't think there's a single other lesbian here.

GRAHAM

The straight boy's found another target.

LOGAN

You're hot. We should totally grind on each other.

CLUB GUY 1

I'll pass.

JULY

You've been staring at him for almost an hour.

GRAHAM

He's a fascinating subject.

(CLUB GUY 2 approaches GRAHAM)

CLUB GUY 2

You wanna come home with me?

GRAHAM

You want herpes?

LOGAN

That's the fifth guy who's hit on Graham tonight.

MELANIE

Why are you counting?

CLUB GUY 2

Come on, I know you want me.

GRAHAM, LOGAN

I need some air.

ALL

I LOVE A BEAT DROP!
DON'T LET THE HEAT STOP!
KEEP UP THE FUN!
KEEP THE LIGHTS BLINDING,
KEEP US ALL GRINDING,
WE'RE NEVER DONE!

DON'T YOU LOVE A FAKE ID?
LIVING LIKE A BRAND NEW YOU!
YOU'RE THE GUY YOU WANNA BE!
AND WHO CARES IF IT'S NOT TRUE?

6. LOOK AT ME / FAKE ID II.. GRAHAM, COMPANY

(Outside Patio of the Club

GRAHAM is there sipping on his drink. LOGAN ENTERS)

GRAHAM

Hey.

LOGAN

Hey.

GRAHAM

Strike out again, straight boy?

LOGAN

"Straight boy," that's me, right? Meanwhile, you turn down every guy in there. You have a boyfriend back home or something?

GRAHAM

Boyfriend? No. I don't hook up. If I took one of those guys home, we'd have sex, he'd make some lame excuse to leave and not stay the night, and never call me again. That's what they do. I'm just an object to them.

LOGAN

Be grateful you're something to them.

GRAHAM

You're – *something* too.

LOGAN

Apparently straight.

GRAHAM

It doesn't matter what I think. Or anyone else. You've just
gotta be yourself.

LOOK AT ME.
DO I LOOK UNHAPPY?
NO, AND I WILL TELL YOU WHY.
I AM WHO I AM
AND DON'T GIVE A DAMN
IF THEY HATE THAT KIND OF GUY.

LOOK AT ME,
DO I FIT SOME MODEL?
NO, THAT NEVER WORKS OUT WELL.
WHEN YOU TRY TO PLEASE,
ALL THAT GUARANTEES
IS THAT YOUR LIFE IS HELL.

IT SEEMS PERFECT AT FIRST GLANCE,
A LIFE YOU WANNA HOOK,
BUT IF YOU COULD BREAK THE TRANCE,
AND REALLY TAKE A

LOOK AT ME,
YOU COULD SEE THERE'S OPTIONS,
THERE'S MORE THAN FITTING IN.
I'M NO PERFECT GAY,
BUT I SURE CAN SAY
THAT I'M HAPPY IN MY SKIN.
'CAUSE AT LEAST I KNOW THE GUY I SEE
WHEN I LOOK AT ME.

LOGAN

Sounds to me like you're just afraid.

GRAHAM

Please. If I wanted one of those guys, I could totally get him.

LOGAN

Pff, big talk.

(CLUB GUY 1 ENTERS)

GRAHAM

Hey. You wanna take me back to your place?

CLUB GUY 1

Uh, sure.

(GRAHAM turns to LOGAN and throws him a set of keys)

GRAHAM

Guess you're driving everyone home. Now, do you still think it's a good idea to be a poser?

(GRAHAM EXITS WITH CLUB GUY 1)

LOGAN

I'll show you who's a poser.

(LOGAN RETURNS

Inside the Club.

A GO-GO BOY, played by BLOG 2, dances on a pole. LOGAN JUMPS UP ON THE POLE and begins dancing with HIM)

MELANIE

I AM A GEEK TYPE.

CORY
FLING OF THE WEEK TYPE.

DANIELLE
ME? I'M A STAR!

JUSTIN
WE ALL DISPLAY IT,

JULY
AND IF WE SAY IT

ALL
THAT'S WHO WE ARE!

DON'T GIVE UP YOUR FAKE ID
DON'T LET PEOPLE STEAL YOUR FUN.
'CAUSE WHAT YOU WILL COME TO SEE
IS THAT DEEP DOWN EV'RYONE –

LOGAN	**DANIELLE**	**ENS.,**
(To GO-GO BOY)	HAS A FAKE ID!	**MELANIE**
Sweet moves		I LOVE A BEAT
right? I could		DROP!
totally be a go-go	A FAKE ID!	DON'T LET THE
boy! Everyone's		HEAT STOP!
staring. We		KEEP UP THE
should totally		FUN!
make out. No, I'm		KEEP THE
serious. I'm a		LIGHTS
great kisser, I		BLINDING,
swear. Look I'll		KEEP US ALL
show you!		GRINDING,
(Tries to kiss		WE'RE NEVER
HIM)		DONE!

ALL

KEEP YOUR FAKE ID!

*(The GO-GO BOY slaps LOGAN.
COLLECTIVE GASP)*

END OF SCENE

SCENE FIVE

(Parking Lot of Portal.

*LOGAN, MELANIE, DANIELLE, JUSTIN,
CORY, and JULY ENTER from the club)*

CORY

I'm traumatized. I'm literally traumatized.

LOGAN

It was just a kiss.

DANIELLE

And a hell of a bitch slap! You know how often you see violence at Portal? Not often, that's the answer.

JULY

It's like you defiled a sacred space.

MELANIE

Guys, come on, was it really that big of a deal?

JUSTIN

Honestly, I'm straight and even I know he fucked up big time.

CORY

Let's get going – wait, where's Graham? He's supposed to drive.

LOGAN

I have the keys. He asked me to drive us.

JULY

On second thought, let's grab a cab. We don't need any of his bad karma polluting us.

CORY

I'll join you. No self-respecting gay guy will talk to me if I'm seen with him.

(DANIELLE, JULY, and CORY START TO LEAVE)

DANIELLE

Let's go, Justin. I'm annoyed and horny.

JUSTIN

Danielle, I don't –

DANIELLE

Less talking, more sexing.

JUSTIN

Not tonight.

(CLUB GUY 2 CROSSES)

DANIELLE

Fine. Hey, hottie, come home with me?

CLUB GUY 2

I'm gay.

DANIELLE

Details, details.

(DANIELLE, JULY, CORY, and CLUB GUY 2 EXIT)

LOGAN

That was literally the worst moment of my life.

MELANIE

So, a bunch of drunk people are mad you got them kicked out of a club. They won't even remember it in the morning.

(GRAHAM ENTERS)

GRAHAM

Where'd everybody go?

LOGAN

They cabbed it. What happened to your hook-up?

GRAHAM

I decided I wasn't in the mood. I took his number. Can I have my keys back?

(LOGAN tosses GRAHAM the keys)

GRAHAM

Ready to head out?

JUSTIN

I'm starved. We should grab Steak 'n Shake.

LOGAN

You know I think I'm gonna grab a cab too –

GRAHAM

Come on, straight boy, I'm not gonna –

LOGAN

It's fine.

MELANIE

I'll come with you.

LOGAN

It's cool, really.

MELANIE

Come on, we'll find a fro-yo place that's open and –

LOGAN

I've gotta figure out my next move.

MELANIE

Then I'll help!

LOGAN

Look, I'm grateful you found the –
(Looking back at GRAHAM)
You know. But your *help* in there… You're a girl. A *straight*
girl. I mean, what do you *know* about being gay?
(Beat, he's gone too far)
That came out wrong, I didn't… I promise, once I figure this
all out, everything is gonna be awesome. We'll have lunch
tomorrow, or maybe dinner, or, well, you know what, I'll text
you. So much to do. But it's all good. It's all good!

(LOGAN EXITS)

GRAHAM

Jeez. He's not the greatest friend on earth.

JUSTIN

You okay?

MELANIE

I'm fine. Of course. Why wouldn't I be?

JUSTIN

I'm sure he's just freaking out and not thinking.

MELANIE

I promise I'm fine. Look, why don't you guys get the car and pick me up by the entrance. Heels, you know.

(JUSTIN hands her his jacket)

JUSTIN

Just in case you get cold.

(JUSTIN and GRAHAM EXIT)

7. ALL FIGURED OUT....................................... MELANIE

MELANIE
(Mocking Logan)
"What do you know about being gay?"
(Bolstering herself)
What do I *know*?

> I KNOW QUANTUM MECHANICS.
> I KNOW HOW AIRPLANES FLY.
> I KNOW HYDRODYNAMICS,
> NINETY DIGITS OF PI.
> I KNOW THIS SITUATION
> WOULD MAKE SO MANY CRY.
> BUT FRANKLY, THAT'S DUMB, AND HERE'S
> WHY:
> IT'S ALL MY ALONE TIME
> THAT FORCED ME TO READ
> AND LED TO THE KNOWLEDGE I TOUT.
> SO, MORE OF MY OWN TIME
> IS JUST WHAT I NEED.
> I'VE GOT IT ALL FIGURED OUT.

MELANIE (CONT)
I KNOW HOW TO COMPILE
PLANS FOR REACHING EACH GOAL.
HOW TO CHOOSE WHAT'S WORTHWHILE,
HOW TO KEEP IN CONTROL.
I KNOW LOGAN HAS COME HERE
WITH A LOST, LONELY SOUL.
THINKING THAT HERE, HE'LL BE WHOLE.
BUT THIS CAMPUS, THESE STUDENTS,
THEY'RE ONLY A BLIP.
THIS ISN'T WHAT LIFE'S ALL ABOUT.
AND I'M BLESSED WITH THE PRUDENCE
TO CHOOSE TO PRESS SKIP,
TO HAVE IT ALL FIGURED OUT.

SO, I DON'T KNOW WHY
THEY THINK I'LL FALL APART HERE.
WHY THEY ACT LIKE
I'VE GOT A BROKEN HEART HERE.
I DON'T NEED CLUBS,
OR LOADS OF FRIENDS,
OR DOUBLE SHOTS OF JACK.
I'M GOOD, HE'S GOOD,
I'M GLAD, WE'RE FINE!
AND BESIDES THAT, HE'LL BE BACK.
HE'LL BE BACK.
HE'LL BE BACK.

NO ONE KNOWS HIM LIKE I DO.
THOUGH HE TENDS TO OBSESS,
GUYS LIKE HIM BY AND BY DO
LET THINGS GO NONETHELESS.
SO, I KNOW NOT TO WORRY.
AND I KNOW NOT TO STRESS.
AND NO WAY WOULD I DARE SECOND GUESS!
'CAUSE I'M WAY MORE THAN SURE WHEN

MELANIE (CONT)
HE GETS PAST THIS PHASE,
WHEN HE 'S FINALLY DONE FREAKING OUT.
WE'LL BE BACK HOW WE WERE THEN,
IN OUR HIGH SCHOOL DAYS.

I KNOW EACH LAW BY NEWTON…
I KNOW HOW TO MAKE CHECKLISTS…
AND I KNOW HE'LL BE BACK, THERE'S NO
DOUBT!
THERE ARE THINGS THAT ENDURE
AND I'M CERTAIN AND SURE
I'VE GOT THEM ALL FIGURED OUT.

END OF SCENE

SCENE SIX

LOGAN

IT'S GONNA BE BETTER.
IT'S GONNA BE BETTER.
I JUST NEED TO FIND THE RIGHT FIT.
SOME CHARACTERISTIC –
THAT'S NOT TOO SIMPLISTIC.
I COULD BE ARTISTIC.
THAT'S IT!
I'M ALLOWED A COUPLE ERRORS.
I'M ALLOWED TO GET THINGS WRONG
'CAUSE I'M BOUND TO GET IT RIGHT
IN NOT TOO LONG.
THEN IT'S GONNA BE BETTER!
IT'S GONNA BE BETTER
WHEN I FIND A WAY TO BELONG.

*(LOGAN EXITS. BLOG POST NOTIFICATION
SOUND. The BLOG TRIO APPEARS)*

BLOG 3

Gay Card Blog post number twenty-seven: perhaps the
opposite of the up-beat Twink is the understated Art Fag.

BLOG 1

Now, before you get offended, it's totally okay to use the
word "fag" here. Its use is ironic. It makes a statement.
Much like the Art Fag himself.

(The Campus Art Museum.

*LOGAN, dressed in dark pretentious clothing, is
with the other MEMBERS OF DIVERSITY
HOUSE. BLOG 1 and 3 become ART FAGS)*

DANIELLE
What's with the funeral clothes?

LOGAN
Oh these? I'm an Art Fag.

JUSTIN
What's an Art Fag?

GRAHAM
Them.

ART FAG 1
THEY DON'T GET HIS SIGNIFICANCE.

ART FAG 3
HE'S IN THE FABRIC OF ART HISTORY.

ART FAG 1
DA VINCI, WARHOL! IT'S SO SAD
THESE IMITATORS CAN'T SEE.

GRAHAM
(To LOGAN)
SO, WHAT MAKES ALL THESE PAINTINGS ART?
THEY'RE HAVING SEX –

DANIELLE
WITH DICKS LIKE CANDY CORN.

LOGAN

NO, SEE THIS STUFF IS CUTTING EDGE.
IT'S ART EMERGING FROM PORN!

(Dead silence)

ART FAG 3

Porn!

ART FAG 1

Porn!

ART FAG 3

Only an imposter would say that.

DANIELLE

Art Fag, huh?

LOGAN

Who wants free cheese? I'll grab free cheese.

(LOGAN SCURRIES AWAY)

MELANIE

I should see if he's okay.

JULY

You can't! You have to see the panorama wing. It'll change
your universe.

GRAHAM

Come on, don't let the straight boy ruin the day.

MELANIE

I guess I will see him back at the house…

(From the other side of the room, LOGAN sees THEM EXIT)

LOGAN

I'VE GOTTA BE BETTER.
I'VE GOTTA BE BETTER.
OKAY, TAKE A BREATH, AND REVIEW.
THE TWINKS WERE TOO CHEEKY.
THE ART FAGS WERE FREAKY.
PERHAPS SOMETHING GEEKY
WOULD DO.
LET HER GO WITH HER NEW BUDDIES.
LET 'EM HANG OUT, I DON'T CARE!
'CAUSE I GUARENTEE THEY'RE GONNA
WANT ME THERE.
WHEN I'VE GOTTEN MUCH BETTER.
IT'S GONNA BE BETTER!
MY LIFE WILL BE AWESOME, I SWEAR!

(LOGAN EXITS. BLOG NOTIFICATION SOUND. The BLOG TRIO APPEARS)

BLOG 2

Gay Card Blog post number forty-four: if you're striving to 'level up' on your quest to discover your inner gay, perhaps the Gay-mer –

BLOG 3

Pun intended and essential.

BLOG 2

– Might be right for you.

(BLOG DISAPPEARS.

The Library.

The MEMBERS OF DIVERSITY HOUSE are there studying)

GRAHAM
Straight people have one name for a hairy guy: hairy. Gay people, we've got bear, otter, cub, how many tiny variations do we need to classify? I like that. I think I'll write that down.

CORY
What do you do with all these fascinating observations?

GRAHAM
I keep a digital journal.

CORY
Can I read it?

GRAHAM
It's private.

(LOGAN, decked out in video game swag, ENTERS with two GAY-MERS)

LOGAN, GAY-MER 1, GAY-MER 2
We'll get top score and never less! We're members of the LGS!

BLOG 3
Just remember, if you want to be a Gay-mer, you better be serious. Newbs are not welcome.

LOGAN

Howdy, housemates. Meet my new friends from the Lakeshore Gaming Society! They're Gay-Mers. Clever, right!

GAY-MER 1

A pleasure.
> *(Resuming a conversation in progress)*
> I LOVE THE LGS, I DO,
> BUT THERE IS ONE THING I CANNOT FORGIVE,
> THEY'RE SO BLIND TO HOW ALL GAMES
> ARE SO HETERONORMATIVE!

GAY-MER 2

NOW COME ON, THAT'S HYPERBOLE.
YOU'RE MAKING JUDGMENTS ON UNFOUNDED WHIMS!
THINK OF PERSONA, MASS EFFECT –

LOGAN

AND NEED I MENTION THE SIMS?

GAY-MER 1

Oh no. He's a casual.

GAY-MER 2

Abort! Abort now!

> *(The GAY-MERS FLEE in one direction,
> LOGAN RETREATS in another)*

MELANIE

I feel bad.

GRAHAM

He's the one who didn't want you around.

CORY

Well, right now I'm your priority. If I don't pass Quantitative Reasoning, they're going to kick me off the swim team.

JULY

You hate swimming.

CORY

But I love swimmers. Pleeeeeaaaasssseee, Melanie.

MELANIE

You're hopeless.

(SHE begins helping HIM)

LOGAN

SAY GOODBYE TO MY HIGHSCHOOL LIFE,
THAT IS WHAT I SAID I'D DO.
WELL, HERE I AM IN MY COLLEGE LIFE,
AND I'VE GOTTA SEE THIS THROUGH.
I'VE GOT THE DRIVE,
A BLOG HERE TO GUIDE ME,
I SHOULD BE DOING FINE!
SO, WHAT THE HECK COULD I BE MISSING?
I NEED A FREAKING SIGN!

(Faint a cappella singing is heard. LOGAN searches for something in the blog. Eureka! HE EXITS.

The Campus Lawn.

The Lakeshore A CAPPELLA GROUP is performing)

A CAPPELLA GROUP
DON'T YOU LOVE A FAKE ID,
LIVING LIKE A BRAND NEW YOU?
PICK ONE UP AND YOU WILL SEE
LIFE IS GREAT FOR PEOPLE WHO
HAVE A FAKE ID.

> *(BLOG NOTIFICATION SOUND. The BLOG
> TRIO EMERGES from the A CAPPELLA
> GROUP)*

BLOG 2
You've heard of gay men's choruses. Do you ever wonder
where those guys come from?

BLOG 1
Chances are, they were A Ca-Homos, gay members of a
cappella groups.

BLOG 3
These people are like campus superstars.

> *(LOGAN ENTERS, dressed in a heavily
> bedazzled knock-off of the A CAPPELLA
> GROUP'S outfit. LOGAN attempts to join their
> performance)*

A CAPPELLA GROUP
I LOVE A BEAT DROP,
DON'T LET THE HEAT STOP,
KEEP UP THE FUN.
KEEP THE LIGHTS BLINDING,
KEEP US ALL GRINDING,
WE'RE NEVER DONE.

LOGAN
DON'T YOU LOVE A FAKE ID,
LIVING LIKE A BRAND NEW YOU?

(The GROUP stares at him)

LOGAN
Sweet pipes, right? Can I join?

SINGER 1
Can you do a backflip?

LOGAN
No.

SINGER 2
Beatbox?

LOGAN
No, but I can sing.

SINGER 3
Please. Singing is the lowest priority.

(They shoo LOGAN away. Suddenly, MELANIE is there)

MELANIE
I liked your performance.

LOGAN
Please, don't make fun of me.

MELANIE
I'm not, I was… I miss you.

LOGAN

Seems like you've been having plenty of fun.

MELANIE

That's not fair.

LOGAN

I'm sorry. Look, I'm tired, I'm stressed –

MELANIE

Are we ever hanging out again?

LOGAN

We'll go to Pride together, how about that?

MELANIE

Okay. Well, you take care of yourself.

LOGAN

Yeah.

(SHE EXITS)

LOGAN

IT'S GONNA BE BETTER.
IT'S GONNA BE BETTER.
THERE'S SO MANY CHOICES I'VE GOT.
THERE'S BEING POETIC,
SOME BRAND-NEW AESTHETIC,
OR MAYBE ATHLETIC, WHY NOT?
SURE, IT'S ALL A BIT CONFUSING,
BEING WHO I WANT TO BE.
BUT IT WON'T BE SO CONFUSING
ONCE I SEE

LOGAN (CONT)
MY WHOLE LIFE GETTING BETTER.
IT'S GONNA BE BETTER
ONCE I'VE FOUND A MUCH BETTER ME.

END OF SCENE

SCENE SEVEN

LOGAN
(Voiceover)
October hit and I was getting desperate. I was ready to try anything. I mean, anything. I even started… exercising!

(The Lake.

CORY and JULY are doing a strange, vaguely pagan ritual-esc dance. LOGAN ENTERS jogging. THEY stop. LOGAN bends down, exhausted for a moment, then suddenly does an over-the-top stretch accompanied by a grunt)

CORY
Are you having some sort of attack?

LOGAN
Training. I'm a Gay Bro now.

JULY
Cory, come help me find some more flowers for my nature shrine. Logan is getting too weird for me.

(CORY and JULY EXIT, dancing and chanting, THEY pass GRAHAM ENTERING, taking notes on his phone)

GRAHAM
People watching never stops being amusing.

(LOGAN returns to stretching, ignoring GRAHAM)

GRAHAM

Impressive game of musical gay boys you've been playing the last few weeks. What are you today?

LOGAN

Gay Bro.

GRAHAM

Ah. Very fitting. I've always thought of you as athletic.

(BROS ENTER)

BRO 1

I could lift that much since I was like twelve, bro.

BRO 2

But could you do it after an all-night kegger?

LOGAN

The Bros have come. Gotta go.

GRAHAM

When was the last time you really worked out?

LOGAN

Last week. Last month. Never. Doesn't matter.

GRAHAM

They're Bros. They work out and they drink. If you're gonna be stupid, at least put a little thought into it.

LOGAN

Okay, I've tried to be nice, but *you*, standing there, lecturing me, it's crap. It's hurtful and spiteful and just crap. So, boo to you! Boo to Diversity House! Boo to everyone!

GRAHAM

Has anyone ever told you that you talk like a dork?

(The GAY BROS have EXITED)

LOGAN

Great, they're gone.

GRAHAM
(Returning to his bench)

A tragedy.

(Beat)

LOGAN

How do you do it?

GRAHAM

Do what?

LOGAN

You walk around telling people you don't give a damn about what they think, and they love you – *want* you. If I did that, no one would ever notice I existed. Must be nice to have it so easy.

9. STEP BACK................................... GRAHAM, LOGAN

GRAHAM

Easy? Come here.

LOGAN

Why?

GRAHAM

Just do it.

(LOGAN JOINS GRAHAM on the bench.
GRAHAM points in the distance)

GRAHAM
LOOK AT THAT GUY, OVER THERE IN THE GYM
SHORTS,
WHAT DO YOU SEE? WHAT DO YOU SEE?

LOGAN
A SWAGGER AND COOLNESS EV'RYBODY LIKE
HIM SPORTS,
THAT'S WHAT I SEE.

GRAHAM
I DON'T AGREE.
HE'S PULLING HIS SHIRT AWAY FROM HIS
CHEST.
THAT MEANS HE THINKS HE'S FAT.
HIS HAIR'S THINNING OUT, HE'S GETTING
DEPRESSED,
THAT'S WHY HE WEARS A HAT.
DID YOU SEE ALL THAT?
CAN YOU SEE ALL THAT?

STEP BACK,
KEEP TRACK.
YOU'LL COMPLAIN, BUT I INSIST:
A POINT OF VIEW
LESS FIXED ON YOU
SHOWS YOU SO MUCH THAT YOU'VE MISSED.

You try.

LOGAN
I don't see how this helps –

GRAHAM

I'm sorry, which one of us has gotten kicked out of a gay bar, a game club, and an a cappella group in the past two months?

LOGAN

OKAY, THERE'S A GIRL AND HER MAKEUP IS
SMEARED UP…

GRAHAM

WHAT DOES THAT MEAN?

LOGAN

WHAT DOES THAT MEAN?
HER GUY WENT AND DUMPED HER, AND SHE
RAN OFF AND TEARED UP!
OPEN AND SHUT!

GRAHAM

POSSIBLY, BUT –

LOGAN

BUT WHAT?

GRAHAM

BUT,
AREN'T THERE HINTS OF SOME STAINS ON HER
SKIRT,
AND A SMIRK RESTRAINING GLEE?

LOGAN

THAT GUY'S MESSY TOO! BET THEY ROLLED IN
THE DIRT –
AND HOOKED UP BEHIND THAT TREE.

GRAHAM
NOW YOU START TO SEE.

LOGAN
WELL, HEY LOOK AT ME!

GRAHAM
STEP BACK.

LOGAN
KEEP TRACK.

GRAHAM
SURE, IT'S NOT HOW MOST EXIST.

LOGAN
SO UNAWARE,

BOTH
THEY NEVER CARE
TO NOTICE WHAT THEY'VE MISSED.

GRAHAM
Danielle, three o'clock.

(DANIELLE ENTERS)

DANIELLE
Have you all seen Justin?

GRAHAM
(Aside to Logan)
She's wearing a new top.

LOGAN
New top Danielle?

DANIELLE

You have eyes, I'm so proud of you.

LOGAN

I don't know how you do it.

DANIELLE

Do what?

LOGAN

Most people wear stuff that bold and – but you pull it off so well. I think you gotta have a certain inner confidence, you know.

DANIELLE

I think you're right. You know, freshman you're growing on me. Maybe you're a little more awesome than I thought. If you see Justin.

(SHE EXITS)

GRAHAM

That's how you do it, "straight boy."

LOGAN

I'm just getting started!

THAT GIRL WHO'S OUTFIT SAYS "QUEEN BEE"
SEEMS LIKE SHE'D ACT ELITE.
BUT SEE HER WITH A GROUP OF FRIENDS,
AND YOU NOTICE THAT SHE'S SWEET.

74

GRAHAM
YOU'D THINK THAT QUIET NERD IS NICE,
BUT HIS TYPING IS A SIGN
OF HOW HE'S SOME WHOLE OTHER PERSON
WHEN HE GETS ONLINE.

LOGAN
THE WHOLE MESS IS CONFUSING WHEN
YOU'RE
TRAPPED INSIDE THE DIN.

GRAHAM
STEPPING BACK IS SO FREEING WHO WOULD
EVER STEP BACK IN?

LOGAN
YOU WOULD NEVER STEP BACK IN.
(Gesturing to Graham)
LOOK AT THAT GUY, LOOKING SO DARN
DISDAINFUL,
WHAT ABOUT HIM?

GRAHAM
(Gesturing to Logan)
WELL, HOW ABOUT HIM, SO DAMN AWKWARD
IT'S PAINFUL,
WHAT ABOUT HIM?

LOGAN
SOME CALL HIM MYSTERIOUS, DISTANT, BUT
COOL.

GRAHAM
SOME THINK HIS ACT IS SAD.

BOTH
THEY BOTH THINK THE OTHER ONE SEEMS
LIKE A TOOL.
BUT HE MIGHT NOT BE SO BAD.

LOGAN
WELL, THIS GUY'D LIKE TO ADD,
THAT SORTA MAKES HIM GLAD.

Well, I should go. The Gay Bros won't wait forever. Thanks
for the advice.

GRAHAM
Logan… same time tomorrow?

(LOGAN nods and EXITS)

GRAHAM
STEP BACK,
KEEP TRACK,
'CAUSE LIFE LOVES TO THROW A TWIST.
YOU'RE WALKING BLIND
AND THEN YOU FIND
THAT RIGHT IN VIEW
IS SOMEONE WHO –
OR SOMETHING THAT YOU MISSED.

9A. WEEKS GO BY........................... GRAHAM, LOGAN

LOGAN
(Voiceover)
And like that, Graham and I were hanging out every day.

(Two weeks later, same spot)

GRAHAM

Look, I'm just saying, I watched a lot of my friends come out, put themselves out there, and get their hearts broken. Gay guys are selfish jerks, that's the way it is.

LOGAN

Okay, yes, *some* are, but you can't possibly think every guy is like that.

GRAHAM

Most of the ones I've met. But, hey, I'm open to changing my mind.

LOGAN

A breakthrough! Gonna add that to your journal?

GRAHAM

I'm taking a break from it. Not as fun as it used to be.

LOGAN
(Voiceover)

I breathed easier around him. Like for once in my life I didn't have to try so hard.

(Another two weeks later)

GRAHAM

So what's the deal with you and Melanie?

LOGAN

We still hang out. Kind of.

GRAHAM

Well, don't lose her. She seems like a good friend.

LOGAN

Yeah, she is.

LOGAN
(Voiceover)

Before I knew it, weeks had past, and I hadn't looked at the blog once.

(Another week later)

GRAHAM

Any plans for Pride?

LOGAN

I don't know. I mean, there's still time.

GRAHAM

Not much. It's next week.

LOGAN

Next week!

(The BLOG TRIO APPEARS)

BLOG 2

You've gotta find out which kind of gay guy you are.

BLOG 3

Only a 5% chance after first semester.

BLOG 1

Tick-tock.

LOGAN
(Voiceover)
After pride, the semester was going to be over. I had to get back to work. But then the strangest thing –

(BLOG NOTIFICATION SOUND)

BLOG TRIO
The Gay Card Blog has been suspended.

(GRAHAM APPROACHES LOGAN, holding a flyer)

GRAHAM
They were passing out Pride flyers. That gay film star Rodrick Richards is gonna be there. Cory was dying. I was thinking maybe we could go together?

LOGAN
Maybe I'm an Otter, or a Gip-ster, or an Ani-gay! Why is every type an animal or a pun?

GRAHAM
Oh god, this again.

LOGAN
I'm missing something fundamental. I mean who cares if I dance well, or know about Warhol's work, or have a mental index of queer characters in video games –

GRAHAM
Logan,

STEP BACK,
KEEP TRACK.

GRAHAM (CONT)

Big picture. What really matters here?

LOGAN

STEP BACK AND SEE
OBJECTIVELY
AND NOTICE WHAT I'VE –

(Beat)

Sex.

GRAHAM

That's a little forward, Logan –

LOGAN

No, no, no, I mean being gay is about sex.

GRAHAM

It's called a sexual orientation so, yeah.

LOGAN

No, look around. Why is everyone putting on all these
personas? What was every person in Diversity House
angling for the second we all met? Why do we go to clubs,
join random groups, wear stupid clothes? Sex. It's so simple.

GRAHAM

Okay, but what does that solve?

(LOGAN grabs the flyer from GRAHAM)

LOGAN
Everything. Graham, I'd love to go to pride with you.

(LOGAN and GRAHAM EXIT)

END OF SCENE

SCENE EIGHT

9B. HEY THERE, MELANIE.............................. JUSTIN

(Diversity House Common Room.

JUSTIN is sitting on the couch, strumming a ukulele. MELANIE ENTERS in a very tacky rainbow outfit. She looks at herself in a nearby mirror)

JUSTIN
(Improvising a song on the ukulele)
HEY THERE, MELANIE.
HOW ARE YOU? START TELLING ME.
THIS DAY'S LIKE WOW,
AND YOU'RE LIKE WOW,
AND... SOMETHING... NOT A FELONY.

MELANIE
It might need a little work. So, do I look properly bedazzled?

JUSTIN
You look great.

MELANIE
It's my first Gay Pride! I'm surprisingly stoked.

JUSTIN
Surprisingly?

MELANIE
Well, yes. It's so quintessentially Diversity House. When I moved in I thought I hated stuff like that.

JUSTIN

What made you change your mind?

MELANIE

I don't know, the events, the people, the comradery of it all –
oh god, I sound like Logan.

JUSTIN

You know, there's an after party tonight. I'm still waiting on
that dance. Or you gonna deny this humble ukulele player
once again?

MELANIE

Well, I didn't know about the ukulele before. The ukulele
changes everything.

JUSTIN

Really?

MELANIE

Absolutely not. Besides, I'm pretty sure Danielle would
disapprove.

JUSTIN

Please, she'll find the only other straight guy at the parade
and – well, we're just hooking up, what did I expect?

MELANIE

I'm sorry.

JUSTIN

It's funny, I think I'm basically the exact person I didn't
want to be in college.

(Beat)

MELANIE

One dance couldn't hurt. Maybe Logan and I will make our
way to the party.

JUSTIN

You and Logan are spending the day together?

MELANIE

Yeah. Just like old times.

(LOGAN and GRAHAM ENTER)

MELANIE

We all set?

LOGAN

Set for what?

MELANIE

To go to Pride together?

LOGAN

Right! Right, of course. Um, Graham's joining us.

GRAHAM

I hope that's cool.

MELANIE

Oh. Yeah… I guess. I just thought –

LOGAN

I promise, it's still one hundred percent Melanie plus Logan
time.

GRAHAM

Just, like, to the power of Graham.

LOGAN

Don't hate me?

10. PERFECT DAY... COMPANY

MELANIE
YOU'RE HERE.
THAT'S WHAT MATTERS.
WHAT MORE
COULD I POSSIBLY WANT?
WHATEVER CAME BEFORE NOW,
TODAY WE'VE GOT IT MADE.
'CAUSE NOTHING –
I MEAN, NOTHING!
WILL RAIN ON MY PRIDE PARADE.

MELANIE, LOGAN
WHATEVER CAME BEFORE NOW,
TODAY WE'VE GOT IT MADE.
'CAUSE NOTHING –
I MEAN, NOTHING!
WILL RAIN ON MY PRIDE PARADE!

(DANIELLE ENTERS, CORY and JULY
FOLLOWING BEHIND)

DANIELLE
Alright, Diversity House, let's go!

CORY
THE TIME IS HERE AND I'M SO DAMN STOKED!
IT'S LIKE GAY CHRISTMAS DAY.

JULY
EROTIC SPIRITS HAVE BEEN EVOKED.
LET'S LET THEM LEAD THE WAY.

DANIELLE

NOW, HONEYS, COME GRAB THAT RAINBOW
SWAG!

CORY, JULY

I'M SO PUMPED! I'VE, LIKE, DIED!

JUSTIN

HEY, SHOULD I MAYBE DRESS UP IN DRAG?

ALL

IT'S ALL COOL AT PRIDE!

ENDLESS FUN,
SHIRTLESS GUYS,
FLYING FLAGS
IN CLOUDLESS SKIES,
EV'RY PROBLEM MELTS AWAY
ON THIS PERFECT DAY.

(Orlando Pride)

MELANIE

So, what should we do? Pole dancing booth, sex toy table,
dunk a drag queen – ?

LOGAN

You know what would be awesome? You should find out
where Rodrick Richards is gonna be. I'm stoked to see him.

MELANIE

Okay. I suppose I can do that. Be right back.

(MELANIE EXITS)

GRAHAM

Alone at last. Not that I have a problem with – listen, I
wanted to ask you – see, I've been having fun these last few
weeks, and I'm realizing that I want, or well, I hope that you
feel –

LOGAN

Cory seems like a real Rodrick Richards fan, right? I mean,
he's gonna make the house go see him.

GRAHAM

Are you listening to me?

(MELANIE RETURNS)

MELANIE

He's on a float near the start of the parade.

LOGAN

Perfect.

*(CORY ENTERS, DANIELLE, JULY, and
JUSTIN TRAILING BEHIND HIM)*

CORY

They're starting the parade! They're starting the parade!

LOGAN

Shall we?

GRAHAM

Logan, I'm trying to talk to you.

LOGAN

I hear you, Graham. We're having fun. So, let's keep having fun.

COME GRAB MY HAND, AND LET'S HEAD DOWN FRONT.

(LOGAN grabs GRAHAM and THEY HEAD TOWARD THE EDGE of the parade track)

GRAHAM

WHY CAN'T I TELL YOU NO?

(MELANIE TRAILS BEHIND)

MELANIE

HEY, GUYS WAIT UP!

GRAHAM

WOW, YOU'RE ON THE HUNT.

LOGAN

DON'T WANNA MISS THE SHOW.

CORY

I SEE THE FLOATS COMING DOWN THE STREET!

DANIELLE, JULY, JUSTIN

GATHER ROUND, FIND A SPOT.

(MELANIE catches up to LOGAN and GRAHAM)

LOGAN, MELANIE, GRAHAM

I SWEAR THIS MOMENT COULD NOT BE BEAT.

ALL
LOOK AT WHAT WE'VE GOT!

ENDLESS FUN,
SHIRTLESS GUYS,
FLYING FLAGS
IN CLOUDLESS SKIES,
EV'RY PROBLEM MELTS AWAY
ON THIS PERFECT DAY.

>*(An elaborate float arrives with RODRICK*
>*RICHARDS on a pedestal, towering over*
>*everything else. The PARADERS SURROUND*
>*the float. During the following, LOGAN JUMPS*
>*on the float, GRABs GRAHAM, and PULLS*
>*HIM UP with him. They dance. LOGAN*
>*becomes more and more provocative as they go)*

ALL
IT'S A DAY TO TAKE A COUPLE CHANCES,
IT'S A DAY TO ACT ON INTUITION.
EYES FRONT, DON'T MAKE ANY BACKWARD
GLANCES,
FREE AND CLEAR OF EV'RY INHIBITION.
JUMP, DANCE, SING, FLIRT, ANYTHING THAT'S
RISKY,
MAYBE EVEN GET A LITTLE FRISKY.
AND BEFORE YOU KNOW IT THINGS ARE
HAP'NING
MAKING PEOPLE SAY –

>*(Suddenly LOGAN grabs GRAHAM and kisses*
>*him)*

ROD

Whew! Now *they're* one hot pair, aren't they, folks?

GRAHAM

Logan?

LOGAN

Trust me.

(*LOGAN kisses him again, more intense*)

ROD

Now, don't get too frisky! You'll make The Rod jealous!

LOGAN

Wouldn't dream of it.

(*Suddenly, LOGAN turns and kisses ROD. He reciprocates*)

JULY

Woah! Is Logan – !

CORY

He's making out with Rodrick Richards!!!

DANIELLE

Alright, I'm saying it. Gay Card returned one hundred times over!

(*ROD grabs a nearby pride flag and drapes it over LOGAN like a royal robe*)

ALL (EXCEPT MELANIE, GRAHAM)
ENDLESS FUN,
SHIRTLESS GUYS,
FLYING FLAGS
IN CLOUDLESS SKIES,
EV'RY PROBLEM MELTS AWAY
ON THIS PERFECT –

NA, NA, NA, NA, NA, NA, NA, NA!
NA, NA, NA, NA, NA, NA, NA, NA!
NA, NA, NA, NA, NA, NA, NA, NA!
YEAH!
ON THIS PERFECT DAY!

> *(PARADERS GATHER around LOGAN on the
> float. GRAHAM BUSTS OUT of the crowd.
> MELANIE CATCHES UP)*

MELANIE
Did you know he was going to do that?

GRAHAM
No. But I guess I shouldn't be surprised.

MELANIE
I'm sorry.

GRAHAM
Yeah. Me too.

> *(LOGAN BREAKS FREE and CROSSES to
> THEM)*

LOGAN
Oh my god, did you see that? Did you see that!

GRAHAM

Hard to miss it.

LOGAN

This random guy just invited me to this exclusive thing at
Portal. Me! Can you believe it? I'm kind of awesome. I
mean, really, I'm kind of awesome.

MELANIE

You're kind of a dick.

LOGAN

Excuse me?

MELANIE

You heard me.

LOGAN

Did I do something?

MELANIE

I mean where to start? For one, you completely ignored me
all day even though this is the first time you've given me
more than ten minutes in over a month. Oh and, you know,
there's also using Graham to make out with some gay porn
star!

LOGAN

Graham's not my boyfriend, I didn't do anything wrong.
Right, Graham?

GRAHAM
(Wounded)

Right.

LOGAN
See.

11. EVERYBODY ELSE / PERFECT DAY II .... MELANIE, LOGAN, GRAHAM, COMPANY

MELANIE
Okay, Logan, I have to say this. I know this is an insanely confusing time for you, and I've tried to be supportive, but ever since you came out, you've been changing and not for the better. I want the guy I knew back.

LOGAN
News flash, Melanie, but this is not about you.

MELANIE
THERE FOR EACH OTHER.
WHAT HAPPENED TO THERE FOR EACH OTHER?
THE BEST FRIEND THAT I ALWAYS KNEW WOULDN'T DO
THE THINGS THAT YOU'VE GONE AND DONE.
HE WOULDN'T MISS WHAT'S IN FRONT OF HIS FACE,
HE WOULDN'T LEAVE HIS FRIENDS DANGLING IN SPACE,
HE WOULDN'T ABANDON HIMSELF JUST TO CHASE
A FEW MEAGER MOMENTS OF FUN.
THERE FOR EACH OTHER.
REMEMBER WE'RE THERE FOR EACH OTHER.
I'M BEGGING YOU DON'T BE SO DESPERATE AND DUMB,
PLEASE, LOOK AT THE GUY YOU'VE BECOME.

LOGAN

OKAY, HERE WE GO, ONE MORE TAKE-MY-
ADVICE SPEECH.
YOU'RE SURE OF YOURSELF, HAVE A MEDAL OR
TWO.
DID YOU EVER THINK, WHILE YOU'RE GIVING
THIS NICE SPEECH,
THAT ALL THAT I WANT IS TO BE MORE LIKE
YOU?
SURE OF WHO I SHOULD BE,
SURE THAT PEOPLE AGREE,
AND BY SOME BIT OF LUCK, THAT'S COME
TRUE.

SO WHY CAN'T YOU LET ME GO BE WHO I AM?
FIN'LY RELAX AND ENJOY WHO I AM?
COME ON, DON'T I GET TO KNOW WHO I AM
JUST LIKE EV'RYBODY ELSE!?

GRAHAM

Logan, you're being an ass. She's trying to look out for you.
I mean, come on, who wants –

LOGAN

AH, YES, HERE'S THE CYNIC WITH MORE
OBSERVATIONS
OF HOW IT'S PATHETIC TO RUN WITH A CROWD.
A PERFECT DUET TO THE NERD'S
DECLARATIONS
OF HOW SHE'S ABOVE ALL I WANT AND SHE'S
PROUD.
GOD, WHAT SAINTS YOU'VE BOTH PLAYED,
I CALL BULL, YOU'RE AFRAID
OF THE HARD TRUTH I'M STATING OUT LOUD,

LOGAN(CONT)

THAT I WANT THE WHOLE WORLD TO LOVE
WHO I AM!
KNOW IT, EMBRACE IT, AND CHEER WHO I AM!
I'M GONNA WALK TALL AND BE WHO I AM,
JUST LIKE EV'RYBODY ELSE!

THIS IS THE GUY WHO DREAMED AND
IMAGINED
HOW IT FEELS WHEN YOU FIN'LY BELONG.
THIS IS THE GUY WHO WILL NOT LOOK
BACKWARDS,
WHEN PEOPLE ARE CALLING HIM HANDSOME
AND STRONG.
PEOPLE CHANGE,
PEOPLE GROW,
PEOPLE LET
OLD THINGS GO,
OR ELSE PEOPLE LET LIFE PASS BY.
I WON'T,
THAT'S NOT THE KIND OF GUY I AM.

GRAHAM

You know what, fine. If that's what you want, go. Live it up.
I hope it's everything you expect.

(GRAHAM EXITS)

MELANIE

You really hurt him.

*(LOGAN STARTS TO HEAD BACK toward the
crowd)*

MELANIE

Logan, stop –

LOGAN

What's your deal, Melanie? You're not my sister, you're not my mother, you're not my girlfriend – god forbid – so what do you care? Leave me alone. Get your own life.

(LOGAN EXITS, leaving MELANIE alone.

Split stage. Graham's Dorm Room.

GRAHAM is typing on his computer)

GRAHAM

Gay Card Blog post number 153. Hello readers. I'm back. Did you miss me? I have to start with an apology. I've been overcomplicating things. A guy I know made an excellent point the other day. Being gay is about sex. Displaying sex, chasing sex, having sex, sex – and absolutely nothing else. And isn't it fucking fantastic. So, embrace it! Enjoy yourselves!

(The GUY from the club ENTERS)

CLUB GUY 1

Glad you called hottie.

GRAHAM
(Still writing)

I sure will.

CLUB GUY 1

What made you change your mind?

GRAHAM

I'VE SPENT SO MUCH TIME TAKING NOTES AND
OBSERVING.
THIS MIGHT BE THE TIME TO PUT THEM TO THE
TEST.
WHAT PURPOSE IS ALL I'VE BEEN WRITING
BEEN SERVING
IF I DON'T GO OUT AND HAVE FUN LIKE THE
REST.

*(LOGAN and MELANIE are alone in their
individual spaces)*

LOGAN, MELANIE

SOMETIMES FRIENDS ARE OUTGROWN,

LOGAN, MELANIE, GRAHAM

I'LL BE FINE ON MY OWN.
MY LIFE'S PERFECT, IT'S GREAT, IT'S THE BEST!

'CAUSE I'M GONNA GO AND EMBRACE WHO I
AM!
CHARGE ON AHEAD AND ENJOY WHO I AM!
I'M SO DAMN SURE OF THE PERSON I AM,
JUST LIKE EV'RYBODY –
JUST LIKE EV'RYBODY –

LOGAN

I'LL BE LIKE EV'RYBODY ELSE!

ALL

ENDLESS FUN,
SHIRTLESS GUYS,
FLYING FLAGS
IN CLOUDLESS SKIES,
EV'RY PROBLEM MELTS AWAY

ENSEMBLE	LOGAN, MELANIE, GRAHAM
NA, NA, NA, NA, NA, NA, NA!	SAY GOODBYE,
NA, NA, NA, NA, NA, NA, NA!	WHAT IS GONE IS GONE.
NA, NA, NA, NA, NA, NA, NA! YEAH!	SAY HELLO, NOW I MUST MOVE ON.

(BLOG NOTIFICATION SOUND. BLOG TRIO APPEARS. LOGAN takes out his phone and begins to read)

BLOG TRIO
New Gay Card Blog post.

ALL
ON THIS PERFECT DAY!

END OF ACT ONE

ACT II

SCENE ONE

(The BLOG TRIO poses center stage)

BLOG 2
LIFE IS BETTER WHEN YOU GET IT ON.
MUSCLES HAVE TO BE FLEXED.

BLOG 1
WE HAVE FUN THEN SAY "BYE-BYE, YOU'RE
GONE!"

BLOG 3
AND WE'RE ON TO THE NEXT.

BLOG 1
WE'RE IN THE MOOD,

BLOG 1, 2
OOO, WHOA,

BLOG 1
FOR PARTIES AND RANDOM SEX.

BLOG 1, 2
IT MIGHT SOUND CRUDE,
BUT WHOA, NO, NO!

*(Suddenly the stage EXPLODES WITH LIGHT
and PEOPLE living it up at a party)*

ALL
WHEN YOU'RE ONE OF US –

GIRL 3
SIPPING ON SANGRIA,

ALL
ONE OF US –

GUY 2
LETTING GRINDING FREE YA,

ALL
ALL GIRLS AND GUYS WISH THAT THEY COULD
BE YA.
YOU'RE ONE OF US!

> *(ALL turn toward center where LOGAN has
> appeared, transformed into the sexiest version of
> himself)*

LOGAN
(Voiceover)
When I came back from winter break, everything was
different. Like really different.

> *(A Bar.*
>
> *PARTY GUY 2 and SILENT GUY (played by
> CORY) JOIN LOGAN)*

PARTY GUY 2
To the sexiest gay boy at Lakeshore College!

LOGAN
I like the sound of that!

(THEY down shots)

PARTY GUY 2

We heard about your stunt at pride. You're a legend.

LOGAN

I *am* kind of awesome.

PARTY GUY 2

So, how do you feel about threesomes?

(Split stage. A Random Dorm Room.

GRAHAM and PARTY GUY 1 have just finished a one-night stand)

PARTY GUY 1

That was hot. How about being regulars?

GRAHAM

One time only.

PARTY GUY 1

Noncommittal. I'm into that.

(GRAHAM CROSSES out of the room, pulls out his phone, and types)

GRAHAM, BLOG 3

The trick to staying on top in the gay world is to be wanted but distant. Have fun, have sex, but never let anyone get too close. That makes you vulnerable.

(BLOG NOTIFICATION SOUND. LOGAN glances at his phone)

LOGAN
I love threesomes. But I do them with tens, not sevens.

(LOGAN retreats. GRAHAM and the BLOG TRIO FORM UP with each other)

GRAHAM, BLOG TRIO
ALL NICE FEELINGS ARE COMPLETELY FAKE,
PUT A SHEILD ON YOUR HEART.
BEST TO MAKE SOMEBODY ELSE'S BREAK,
THAN HAVE YOURS TORN APART.

LOGAN, GRAHAM
TIME ROLLS ALONG.

BLOG TRIO
OOO, WHOA!

LOGAN, GRAHAM
YOU HAVE WHAT YOU THINK YOU WANT.
BUT WERE YOU WRONG?

ALL
OOO, WHOA! NO, NO!

WHEN YOU'RE ONE OF US –

GUY 1
HOT AS ABERCROMBIE,

ALL
ONE OF US –

GUY 2
THEY KNOW WHO THE BOMB BE.

ALL
BOYS WANT YOUR FLESH
LIKE A HUNGRY ZOMBIE.
YOU'RE ONE OF US!

(On a dance floor.

PARTY GUY 1 is grinding on LOGAN)

PARTY GUY 1
My car's really roomy.

LOGAN
Oh. You know, I've got an early class, so I shouldn't –

PARTY GUY 1
Huh. Guess my friends were right about you.

LOGAN
What do you mean?

PARTY GUY 1
They say you're a tease. You never fuck anyone.

(Split stage. A Random Dorm Room.

*GRAHAM, PARTY GUY 2, and SILENT GUY
are finishing a hookup)*

PARTY GUY 2
You know Logan?

GRAHAM
Unfortunately.

PARTY GUY 2
We tried to do a three-way with him. Didn't happen. I heard a rumor he's secretly still a virgin. Can you imagine?

(GRAHAM CROSSES out of the room, typing on his phone)

GRAHAM, BLOG 3
A Gay Card can be lost just as quickly as it was earned. One hint that it's not truly deserved, and it's gone in a flash.

LOGAN
Your friends are wrong about me. I just don't do cars. Take me back to your place.

ALL
WHAT'S SO WRONG WITH HOW WE CHOOSE TO LIVE?
THEY SAY BE ANGELS INSTEAD.
BUT EACH NIGHT I SWEAR WE GIVE AND GIVE,
BOTH IN TIPS AND IN BED.

GUY 3
SO DIVE RIGHT IN,

LOGAN
DIVE RIGHT IN…

ALL
OOO, WHOA!

GUY 3
WE SWEAR YOU WON'T WANT TO LEAVE.

LOGAN
I DON'T WANT TO LEAVE!

GIRL 2, GUY 2
INDULGE EACH SIN,

LOGAN
INDULGE EACH SIN.

ALL
OOO, WHOA, WHOA, WHOA!

WHEN YOU'RE ONE OF US –

GUY 1
GETTING D. AND B.J.S,
ONE OF US –

GIRL 3
BIRTHDAY SUIT'S YOUR P.J.S,

ALL
YOU'RE TURNING TRICKS LIKE YOU'RE HOTTIE
D.J.S!
YOU'RE ONE OF US!

(PARTY GUY 1 is undressing LOGAN)

LOGAN
Wait. Stop. I'm sorry, I just – I can't.

GUY 1
God damn it. What's your deal? STD? Religious?

LOGAN
I – I don't know. It just doesn't feel right. I'll go.

(LOGAN CROSSES TO

Diversity House Common Room)

GRAHAM

Hey.

LOGAN

Hey.

GRAHAM

Getting in pretty late.

LOGAN

I always wanted to stay out 'til morning. Guess you've gotten over your aversion to hooking up.

GRAHAM

Guess there's no doubt you're gay now.

LOGAN

Was he any good?

GRAHAM

Yeah. It was fun. Yours?

LOGAN

The best. Like always.

GRAHAM

Well, guess I should get packed. The spring break bus will be leaving soon. Don't wanna make the house wait on us.

(GRAHAM EXITS)

LOGAN
(Voiceover)
So, like that it was spring break. I had been having the best damn semester I could have asked for. So why was it feeling so... empty?

LOGAN
OUT OF YOUR MIND.
DON'T THINK ABOUT HIM.
HIS LITTLE SMIRK?
NO, LET IT GO.
OUT OF YOUR MIND.
YOU'RE FINE WITHOUT HIM.
WHAT COULD HAVE BEEN?
NO NEED TO KNOW.
LEAVE IT BEHIND
OR YOU WILL FIND
IT'S GONNA DRIVE YOU
OUT OF YOUR MIND.

> *(DIVERSITY HOUSE MEMBERS all ENTER, bags in hand, ready for spring break. The BLOG TRIO surrounds LOGAN)*

ENSEMBLE
WHOA WHOA WHOA!
NOW YOU'RE ONE OF
US,
GLAD WE COULD
CONVERT YA!
STICK WITH US!
AND WE'LL SOON
PERVERT YA!
THERE'S NOT A SOUL
THAT CAN EVER HURT
YA!
YOU'RE ONE OF US!
YOU'RE ONE OF US!

LOGAN
LEAVE IT BEHIND,
THE PAST WAS SHODDY.
SOMEHOW YOU'LL FIND
YOU CAN FEEL
NAUGHTY.
OUT OF YOUR MIND
AND IN YOUR BODY.

END OF SCENE

SCENE TWO

LOGAN
(Voiceover)
Spring break could not have come sooner. Every year, the house went to a place on the beach that was pretty far from the normal spring break hot spots. I thought I was safe for the week.

(Outside the Vacation House, Near the Beach.

MELANIE STEPS OUT of the house and breathes in the fresh air. SHE SITS DOWN and pulls out a book. JULY BURSTS OUT of the house)

JULY
The sea spirits are beckoning, Melanie. Come for a swim?

MELANIE
I'm all set with my book.

JULY
You've been cooped up in your room studying all semester.

MELANIE
Why don't you swim with Cory?

JULY
He's preoccupied.

(LOGAN ENTERS, CORY TRAILING BEHIND)

CORY

Thank god for the beach. You looked great with your shirt off, Logan.

LOGAN

Thanks, Cory.

CORY

Have I told you how cute you are?

LOGAN

Only once every day since November. I miss when you were hitting on Graham.

CORY

Please, Graham is old news.

LOGAN

Come swim with us, July?

CORY

I was hoping for some privacy.

LOGAN

I wasn't.

(DANIELLE ENTERS from the house)

DANIELLE

Fine, Justin, just fine! Who wants you anyway!
(Noticing the attention she's drawn)
What are you all staring at? I want swimming, stripping, and skinny dipping right now!

(And with that, DANIELLE, CORY, JULY, and LOGAN EXIT. JUSTIN ENTERS)

JUSTIN

All clear?

MELANIE

Appears so. Everything okay?

JUSTIN

I did it.

MELANIE

Did what?

JUSTIN

We're done. Finito. Over.

MELANIE

That's – wow, that's –

(GRAHAM ENTERS from the house)

GRAHAM

Hey, Melanie – and Justin. Thought you'd be swimming or tanning or whatever you do.

JUSTIN

There's a red flag on the beach. "Warning: angry ex in water."

MELANIE

You okay, Graham?

GRAHAM

It's no biggie. I'll find you later.

MELANIE

I'm here now.

GRAHAM

Well – I was just wondering if you've talked with Logan lately.

JUSTIN

I can split if you two –

MELANIE

I'm taking the noble gas approach with Logan: one hundred percent nonreactive.

GRAHAM

Right. That's what I figured. Okay, I'll see you.

MELANIE

You're not still hung up on him or something, are you?

GRAHAM

Me? Nah. No. It's just – you know – he can be all naïve and stuff, and with all the guys he's been with lately – but I guess it's fine 'cause I heard a rumor he wasn't really going through with it anyway, so I'm probably worried for nothing. If that rumor is true. But you wouldn't know.

MELANIE

Not having sex, and then lying and saying he's having sex? Sounds like Logan.

GRAHAM

So, you think it's true?

MELANIE

You *are* still hung up on him.

GRAHAM

Please, he's a poser, a liar, an ass –

112

MELANIE

Exactly. So, walk away. He's not worth it. Believe me, I know.

GRAHAM

That's what I'm doing.

MELANIE

Good.

GRAHAM

I'm serious.

MELANIE

Good.

GRAHAM

Okay, good talk. Guess I'll see you later. Enjoy your book.

(GRAHAM EXITS)

JUSTIN

I'm sorry about Logan.

MELANIE

I'm not. I've moved on. What were we talking about?

JUSTIN

It's not important.

MELANIE

Breaking up with Danielle, that was it.

JUSTIN

You really care about him, don't you?

MELANIE

You're getting off topic –

JUSTIN

For what it's worth, I don't think you should give up on him so easily. When you have something special you shouldn't let it slip away.

MELANIE

Nice sentiment, but Logan really hurt me.

JUSTIN

I get that.

(JUSTIN goes behind a piece of furniture...)

MELANIE

All evidence points to the definitive conclusion that he doesn't care one bit about me. And after all, if you look at our history logically –

(...and JUSTIN pulls out his Ukulele)

13. A BREAK.. JUSTIN

MELANIE

Oh, not this again.

JUSTIN

This again.

JUSTIN

GIVE THE GUY A BREAK.
HEY, THAT'S WHAT THIS WEEK IS FOR.
HAVE WAY MORE SUN,

JUSTIN (CONT)
HAVE WAY MORE FUN,
HAVE WAY LESS TWO BEST FRIENDS AT WAR.
YES, HE MADE A MISTAKE,
WE ALL MAKE THEM NOW AND THEN.
BUT, GIVE THE GUY A BREAK
AND THEN TRY TO START AGAIN.

MELANIE
Well, you're definitely improving, but –

JUSTIN
WE ALL NEED A BREAK,
HEY, BELIEVE ME, I SHOULD KNOW:
THE HIGH SCHOOL JOCK
WHO WALKED THE WALK,
NEVER LETTING ALL HIS FEELINGS SHOW,
WHO JOINED THIS HOUSE TO MAKE
A NEW START, OUTSIDE AND IN,
'CAUSE WE ALL NEED A BREAK,
FREEING US FROM WHO WE'VE BEEN.

AND IT'S OKAY TO CHANGE
YOUR CLOTHES, YOUR HABITS, HOW YOU ACT.
AND WHO YOU ARE IS MORE
A GUESSING GAME THAN SOLID FACT.
AND IT'S OKAY TO FIGHT,
AND IT'S OKAY TO MAKE AMENDS,
AND IT'S OKAY TO WISH
THAT YOU TWO WERE MORE THAN FRIENDS.

MELANIE
I don't know if I like this song.

JUSTIN
GIVE YOURSELF A BREAK.
YOU COULD USE A BIT LESS STRESS.
DON'T LOOK SO GRIM,
'CAUSE LOVING HIM,
DOESN'T MEAN YOU'RE SOMEHOW ANY LESS.
I MEAN, FOR GOODNESS SAKE,
YOU'RE A CATCH, A SCORE, A STEAL.
SO, GIVE YOURSELF A BREAK
FROM DENYING WHAT YOU FEEL.
GIVE YOURSELF A BREAK
FROM DENYING WHAT YOU FEEL.

You think I'm in love with Logan?

JUSTIN
It's okay.

MELANIE
That's not who I am. You're wrong.

(SHE kisses JUSTIN)

MELANIE
Proof enough for you?

JUSTIN
I don't know… I think you should prove me wrong again
just to be sure.

*(THEY kiss again. LOGAN ENTERS as they do,
seeing. HE TURNS TO LEAVE, but DANIELLE
and the rest of DIVERSITY HOUSE ENTER)*

DANIELLE

All right, Diversity House, it's sunset already and I'm only tipsy. We need to fix that! Games! Games somebody!

LOGAN

Ring of Fire?

JULY

Never Have I Ever?

CORY

Truth or Dare!

DANIELLE

Not a drinking game.

CORY

Anything can be a drinking game. Drink when you truth or dare someone, drink when you're truth-ed or dared. You can switch from a truth to a dare or a dare to a truth, but you have to beat the other person in a waterfall.

DANIELLE

That sounds like a terrible drinking game.

> (CORY whispers something in DANIELLE'S ear)

DANIELLE

You little man-whore. That sounds like a great drinking game. We're playing.

JULY

Wait, what?

CORY

I'm first. Logan, truth or dare?

LOGAN

Dare.

CORY

I dare you to make out with me.

LOGAN

Should have seen that one coming.

(LOGAN does so)

LOGAN

July, truth or dare?

JULY

Truth.

LOGAN

If you could have sex with any girl here, who would it be?

JULY

Well… Melanie. Danielle don't hate me.

DANIELLE

You wear feathers on a regular basis. Obviously, your taste is questionable.

JULY
(A bit insulted)

Danielle, truth or dare?

DANIELLE

Truth.

JULY

How many guys have you slept with since you started hooking up with Justin?

DANIELLE

None. I just like to look. Don't assume things. Logan –

LOGAN

Hey, I already went this round.

DANIELLE

Not a rule we established. Right, Cory?

CORY

Right.

DANIELLE

Truth or dare?

LOGAN

Dare.

DANIELLE

Okay. I dare you to go upstairs and have sex with Cory.

LOGAN

That's way too far. Is that allowed? I don't think that's allowed.

DANIELLE

Were there more ground rules that I missed?

GRAHAM

Come on, Danielle.

DANIELLE

What? He hooks up with a new guy every night.

14. FAKE ID (REPRISE)................. DIVERSITY HOUSE

LOGAN

I… well… sure I do. But they're all hotter than him. I'm switching. Truth.

> *(Suddenly, a SPOTLIGHT hits the center of the circle and only dim red light illuminates the edges. DANIELLE steps into the spot)*

DANIELLE

Waterfall then. But I warn you, I'm the master.

> *(LOGAN STEPS in the spot. They circle one another)*

CORY, JULY, JUSTIN, GRAHAM, MELANIE
TENSION IS RIFE, BOY,
CHUG FOR YOUR LIFE, BOY,
THINK WHAT'S AT STAKE.
ALL THAT YOU'VE STRIVED FOR
WILL BE DEPRIVED FOR
ONE SMALL MISTAKE.

> *(CORY RUNS INTO THE CIRCLE, hand up, and drops it)*

CORY

Go!

> *(LOGAN and DANIELLE chug their drinks)*

CORY, JULY, JUSTIN, GRAHAM, MELANIE
DON'T GIVE UP YOUR FAKE ID.
DON'T LET PEOPLE STEAL YOUR FUN.
'CAUSE WHAT YOU WILL COME TO SEE
IS THAT DEEP DOWN EV'RYONE –

LOGAN
I win!

(THE LIGHTS RETURN TO NORMAL)

DANIELLE
Sorry, Cory, I tried. Okay, truth. How about some delicious details? Which guys at Lakeshore have you fucked?

LOGAN
Which guys have I –

DANIELLE
Yes. Which guys have you fucked?

LOGAN
Justin, truth or dare?

DANIELLE
That's not how it works, freshman –

LOGAN
Justin, truth, were you and Melanie making out five minutes ago?

MELANIE
Logan!

JUSTIN
Dude!

DANIELLE

She's the one? Huh. Guess the nerd turned out to be as big a
slut as the rest of us.

MELANIE

Take that back.

DANIELLE

Relax. It's not like I care. I *am* curious why freshman here is
so desperate to not answer my truth. What's the dirty little
secret?

MELANIE

The secret is Logan hasn't slept with anyone.

GRAHAM

Melanie!

MELANIE

This whole persona he's got going on is completely fake.
Well, except the part where he hurts his friends. That part's
real.

(MELANIE STORMS OFF)

END OF SCENE

SCENE THREE

(A Bedroom in the Vacation House.

MELANIE ENTERS, FOLLOWED BY LOGAN.
MELANIE starts packing)

LOGAN
You had no right to say that!

MELANIE
Yes, well neither did you.

LOGAN
Where are you going?

MELANIE
Back to Lakeshore. Spending Spring Break here suddenly sounds excruciating.

LOGAN
How the hell are you going to get there?

MELANIE
Bus, train, jet ski if necessary!

LOGAN
No, no, no, no, no, you can't leave! You have to tell them you were lying. You have to tell them you were mad and being spiteful.

MELANIE
Spiteful? Spiteful! I've done everything I could for you. I moved into Diversity House *for you*. I found the Gay Card Blog *for you*. I endured your shallow little quest *for you*!

MELANIE (CONT)

And for once, I do something for me, and you take that away from me. Because god forbid Logan Kappler ever lets his best friend be happy.

LOGAN

How have I ever stopped you from being happy?!

MELANIE

I love you, okay!!! There, I said it. I know it's stupid, I know it's pointless, but I do. I love you. Always have.

LOGAN

Well, that's not my fault, Melanie.

15. EXTRANEOUS... MELANIE

MELANIE
(Cold, finished)
I think you should leave, Logan.

LOGAN

That's it? Leave. That's all our friendship – ?

MELANIE

IN MATH,
WHEN YOU HAVE A PROBLEM,
THERE'S A QUICK WAY TO RESOLVE IT.
YOU READ THE PROBLEM,
DRAW A PICTURE,
TAKE SIMPLE STEPS TO SOLVE IT.
YOU MAKE A TABLE,
LIST THE FACTORS,
WORK THEM MATHEMATICALLY,
BUT MOST IMPORTANTLY:
YOU LOOK TO SEE

MELANIE (CONT)
IF THERE MIGHT BE
ANYTHING
EXTRANEOUS.

LOGAN
Melanie. Melanie, please…

MELANIE
IN LIFE,
WHEN YOUR FRIEND'S A BUTTHEAD,
THERE'S AN EASY WAY TO FIX IT.
YOU SET YOUR LIFE GOALS,
MAKE A MODEL,
WHAT DOESN'T FIT, YOU NIX IT.
YOU TAKE WHAT'S HELPFUL,
LOSE THE BAGGAGE,
WORK YOUR LIFE OUT LOGICALLY,
BUT MOST IMPORTANTLY:
YOU DON'T DEFEND
A SPITEFUL FRIEND
WHO'S NOTHING BUT
EXTRANEOUS.

LOGAN
Fine. Fine, I'll fix it myself. Screw you.

(LOGAN EXITS)

MELANIE
THOUGH SO MUCH FEELS ESSENTIAL –
OUR DRIVES TO BAYPOINT HEIGHTS,
OUR CONFIDENTIAL MOONLIGHT TALKS,
OUR STUPID MOVIE NIGHTS –
FACT IS THE MILLION THINGS WE SHARED

MELANIE (CONT)
HAVE SLOWLY DROPPED TO NONE,
AND OUR ONCE ESSENTIAL FRIENDSHIP
IS OUTDATED, FINISHED, DONE.

IN TIME,
ALL THINGS HAVE AN ENDING,
BUT THE TRICK IS TO ACCEPT IT.
A FRIENDSHIP PASSES,
THAT STUFF HAPPENS,
IT'S DUMB TO WISH YOU KEPT IT.
YOU CHANGE YOUR MODEL,
MAKE ADJUSTMENTS,
LIVE YOUR LIFE ADAPTIVELY,
BUT MOST IMPORTANTLY:
YOU SAY GOODBYE
TO ANY GUY
WHO MAKES YOU FEEL…
EXTRANEOUS.

END OF SCENE

SCENE FOUR

15A. POST NUMBER 180.................... INSTRUMENTAL

(The BLOG TRIO APPEARS in SPOTLIGHT)

BLOG TRIO
Gay Card Blog post number 180. The bottom line.

BLOG 1
There is no love.

BLOG 3
Don't look for it.

BLOG 2
There's only being wanted and not being wanted.

BLOG 3
Accept that.

BLOG 1
The game can be fun.

BLOG 3
Enjoy it.

BLOG 2
You don't need anything more.

16. FOLLOW ME (REPRISE)...................... BLOG TRIO

(The Beach at Night.

LOGAN is PULLING CORY behind a rock)

CORY

Out here in the open? Someone could see.

LOGAN

That's the point.

BLOG 2

REMEMBER THE WAY THINGS WERE.

CORY

You ready for this, tiger?

BLOG 1

YOU CAN'T LET THAT REOCCUR.

LOGAN

Ready as I'll ever be.

    (THEY undress one another, slowly, during the following)

BLOG 3

HEY, BUDDY YOU'VE COME SO FAR,
HOW COULD THIS BE WRONG?

BLOG 2, 3

PROVE WHICH KIND OF GUY YOU ARE,
AND YOU'LL FEEL LIKE YOU BELONG.

BLOG 1

SO, NEED I ILLUSTRATE?

BLOG TRIO
GRAB A CONDOM AND FOLLOW ME!
TAKE THIS HOTTIE, BOY, AND TELL HIM "I'M
YOURS."
YOU COULD USE A NEW P.O.V.,
LIKE ON YOUR BACK OR ON ALL FOURS –

(GRAHAM ENTERS. The BLOG TRIO
DISAPPEARS)

GRAHAM

Stop!

LOGAN

We're busy.

GRAHAM

Cory, give us a minute –

CORY

Yeah, right –

GRAHAM

Now!

CORY

Jeez. Okay, okay.

(CORY EXITS)

LOGAN

What is it, Graham?

GRAHAM

Cory? I mean, come on.

LOGAN

You did not come all the way out here just to judge me.

GRAHAM

Why are you doing this?

LOGAN

Because I want to.

GRAHAM

Because you have to?

LOGAN

I don't need to justify myself to you.

GRAHAM

No. No, you don't.

LOGAN

Well, if we're done here –

GRAHAM

I have to know something. Back in November, at Pride, when you kissed me, did you feel – was it all just part of some plan or…?

LOGAN

You're one giant wall, Graham. Even if I did feel something, how could I ever hope to break through?

17. AFRAID.. GRAHAM

GRAHAM

You couldn't. But you did.

GRAHAM (CONT)

I HATED TO FOLLOW THE TRENDS,
I HATED TO STAY OUT TOO LATE,
I HATED TO PARTY WITH FRIENDS,
OR GO OUT ON EVEN ONE DATE.
I HATED THE CLUBS,
THE FLIRTS AND THE SNUBS,
I HATED THE WHOLE DAMN CHARADE,
'TIL YOU CAME ALONG AND SAID,
"YOU'RE JUST AFRAID."

I HATED THE WAY YOU JUMPED IN,
I HATED HOW YOU NEVER QUIT,
HOW YOU WERE DETERMINED TO WIN,
HOW YOU WERE SO CERTAIN YOU'D FIT.
I SWORE YOU WERE DUMB
SINCE I HAD BECOME
SO SURE OF THE CHOICES I MADE,
AND NEVER CONSIDERED THAT I
WAS JUST AFRAID.

BUT AS I'VE SEEN YOU FLIRT,
AS I'VE WATCHED YOU DANCE,
THOUGH A PART OF ME HURT,
ANOTHER SAW A CHANCE
TO BE THE GUY
WHO SAYS I'LL TRY
AND LEAPS INTO THE FRAY,
TO NOT HOLD BACK,
LET ARMOR CRACK,
BE BRAVE ENOUGH TO SAY

I LOVE HOW YOU LIGHT UP A ROOM,
I LOVE HOW YOU DANCE UNTIL DAWN,
AND WHEN I GO ALL DOOM AND GLOOM,
YOU SMILE AND THAT FEELING IS GONE.

GRAHAM (CONT)
I'VE CLUNG TO MY PART,
I'VE WALLED OFF MY HEART,
BUT I SWEAR I'LL BREAK DOWN THAT
BLOCKADE.

I DON'T WANNA LET WHAT WE STARTED JUST
FADE,
I KNOW EACH MISTAKE HAS A PRICE TO BE
PAID,
BUT I CANNOT JUST STAY IN THE PLACE THAT
I'VE STAYED,
SO PLEASE WON'T YOU SHOW ME HOW NOT
TO BE AFRAID?

*(LOGAN grabs GRAHAM and kisses him.
LIGHTS OUT)*

END OF SCENE

SCENE FIVE

LOGAN
(Voiceover)

That night Graham and I – you know. And afterwards, I was lying there. Graham had already fallen asleep. He was beautiful. I laid there. I breathed in. I breathed out. And I realized I didn't want to be anywhere else. My journey created that connection – and it also broke it.

(A Bedroom in the Vacation House.

GRAHAM and LOGAN are in bed together. LOGAN is asleep. GRAHAM wakes up and soaks in the moment. Suddenly, an idea strikes, he pulls out his phone, and CROSSES out of the bed. BLOG TRIO APPEARS)

BLOG TRIO
Gay Card Blog post number 181: an addendum.

BLOG 1
I've read some of your comments over the last few months.

BLOG 2
Some of you say I'm growing cynical.

BLOG 3
Yeah, maybe.

BLOG 2
But there are times – times like now, when all that cynicism goes away.

BLOG 3

Most of the time, life is what you go and take.

BLOG 1

But sometimes, life sneaks in and finds you.

BLOG TRIO

And all you can do is savor that moment for all it's worth.

(GRAHAM hits post. BLOG NOTIFICATION SOUND. LOGAN stirs. GRAHAM scrambles to put his phone away, but LOGAN is already awake. The BLOG TRIO DISAPPEARS)

LOGAN

Good morning.

GRAHAM

Hey.

LOGAN

It's early. Come back to bed.

GRAHAM

Sure.

(GRAHAM RETURNS to bed)

LOGAN

What were you doing?

GRAHAM

Oh – you know, checking my grades from midterms. All A's like I figured.

LOGAN

But they don't get posted until next week.

GRAHAM

Yeah – well – they're gonna be A's so –

LOGAN

Everything's okay, right?

GRAHAM

Yeah! No worries. Let's just cuddle for a bit.

(THEY do. But then LOGAN can't hold back)

LOGAN

You weren't – like – messaging another guy, were you?

GRAHAM

No, of course not. Why would you think that?

LOGAN

It's just, that's what you've been doing since November, so why would you stop just 'cause of one –

GRAHAM

I told you last night how I feel.

LOGAN

You're being a little defensive for someone who has nothing to hide.

GRAHAM

Logan, just drop it, okay?

LOGAN

Then show me what you were doing.

GRAHAM

If we're gonna get anywhere together, you have to trust me.

LOGAN

Well, boyfriends don't keep secrets.

GRAHAM

Okay.

(GRAHAM grabs his phone and shows LOGAN)

LOGAN

I don't understand.

GRAHAM

Look it's just something I do for fun, it doesn't –

LOGAN

You write the Gay Card Blog?

GRAHAM

Yes, but –

LOGAN

You?! I've been following this blog since August.

GRAHAM

You've been following the blog since – oh shit –

LOGAN

You stood there and judged me for what I was doing, but looks like you had already been there, done that!

GRAHAM

No, you don't get it –

LOGAN

I mean, the shit you've been pulling since Pride is one thing, but this has been around way longer. That whole time you were partying, and fucking, and judging, and leading this whole double life, and that's when you fell in love with me? Or did you? I mean, you should clarify which Graham is the one who told me he loved me last night –

GRAHAM

I do love you –

LOGAN

How can I believe you? How can I believe anything you say when there is this whole other person that you've been hiding?

GRAHAM

I never did the things in that blog. At least not 'til after Pride.

LOGAN

You're a liar.

GRAHAM

The blog was a joke, Logan! A parody, a commentary, a way of exposing how fucked up we can be. That was pretty obvious. If you followed it like a bible, congratulations: you're the biggest idiot in all of Central Florida!

LOGAN

Get out! We're done here.

(GRAHAM OPENS THE DOOR to leave. CORY, JULY, and DANIELLE are there)

JULY

You okay, Logan?

CORY

Graham, you're still here? Oh my god, you guys didn't –

DANIELLE

Well, what do you know, you *are* a man-whore, Logan. Good for you.

GRAHAM

Yeah, good for him, right?
  (Grabs a nearby slip of paper, and writes something on it)
 I think we need to make this official, guys.
        (Hands the paper to LOGAN)
You wanted your Gay Card, that's what the blog was all about. Here. Congratulations. You got it. You finally belong. And that's really all that matters, isn't it?

> *(GRAHAM STORMS OUT. The REST TRY TO GATHER around LOGAN and get the juicy details, but HE WALKS AWAY. Alone, he looks down at his "Gay Card")*

18. THE KIND OF GUY I AM............................ LOGAN

LOGAN
(Quietly, wounded)

Fuck you, Graham.
            (Lashing out)

Fuck you!

THIS IS THE GUY WHO WANTED A NEW LIFE,
WHO WENT OUT AND FOUND WHO HE WAS.
THIS IS THE GUY WHO'S HAPPY HE DID IT,
ENORMOUSLY HAPPY BECAUSE –
WELL, BECAUSE –

Ugh!

YOU SAID THAT I LIGHT UP A ROOM –

Yeah, right!

YOU LOVE HOW I DANCE UNTIL DAWN –

What a joke!

WITHOUT YOU MY LIFE CAN RESUME.
AND TRUTH IS I'M GLAD THAT YOU'RE –

I mean,

LOOK AT ME!
LOOK WHERE I AM NOW!
IT'S PERFECT AS CAN BE!
SURE, YOU CAN MAKE FUN
OF THE THINGS I'VE DONE,
BUT COME ON LOOK AT ME!
COME ON LOOK AT ME!

I DON'T WANT YOU,
I DON'T NEED YOU,
I AM GLAD THAT I BELONG.
IF YOU THINK THAT
YOU CAN HURT ME
WELL, I'M SORRY BUT YOU'RE WRONG.
I MEAN, WHO FINDS THEIR TRUE LOVE
AT EIGHTEEN?
WHO REALLY WANTS TO DO LOVE
WHEN THEY'VE SEEN

LOGAN (CONT)

ENDLESS FUN,
SHIRTLESS GUYS?
EV'RY DAY IS
CLEAR BLUE SKIES!
LET THE PROBLEMS MELT AWAY!

I SAY NA, NA, NA, NA, NA, NA, NA, NA!
NA, NA, NA, NA, NA, NA, NA, NA!
NA, NA, NA, NA, NA, NA, NA, NA!
NA, NA, NA, NA, NA – !

THIS IS THE GUY WHO FIVE MINUTES AGO,
FELT HE WAS COMPLETELY CONTENT,
THIS IS THE GUY WHO FIVE MINUTES LATER,
FEELS SO DAMN CONFUSED AS TO WHAT ALL
THAT MEANT.
BECAUSE THERE IN THAT BED,
ALL THE OLD FEARS WERE DEAD,
BUT NOW THAT HE'S SAID HIS GOODBYE,
I'M LEFT
TO FACE THE KIND OF GUY I AM.

END OF SCENE

SCENE SIX

(Outside the Vacation House, just before sunrise.

MELANIE is waiting, a suitcase by her side.
LOGAN enters, also holding a suitcase)

LOGAN

Hey.

MELANIE

Logan.

LOGAN

You're still here.

MELANIE

First bus doesn't leave for an hour.

LOGAN

Listen, you should stay. I'm getting out of here anyway. As
for back at school –

MELANIE

The problem's already been solved, you don't have to worry.
I'm leaving Diversity House. It was never my thing anyway.
I was only there for you.

LOGAN

I'm sorry about that. I'm sorry I dragged you along on my
whole stupid quest. I'm sorry that I never stopped thinking
of myself long enough to see how you felt.

MELANIE

If we're being honest, I think I loved you because it was
safe. Because deep down, I knew you'd never love me back.
This year I wasn't safe, and I kind of liked it. That's what's
so confusing.

LOGAN

You'll figure it out. You're mathlete Melanie! You've got a
plan. You know the formulas, the variables, the constants –

19. PLAYING PRETEND................. MELANIE, LOGAN

MELANIE

I'm not sure there are constants, Logan. We both thought we
knew what we wanted and who we were; and what are we
now? The wild gay boy who everybody loves? The smart
girl who's got it all figured out?

ARE WE PLAYING PRETEND?
LITTLE KIDS ACTING
LIKE WE ARE ALL GROWN?
PLAYING PRETEND,
PUTTING ON FACES
TO BRAVE THE UNKNOWN?
I BELIEVED THAT ONE DAY I'D GROW UP,
I'D BE SMART, AND TALL, AND SURE,
BUT IF WE'RE SIMPLY PLAYING PRETEND,
THEN WE'LL NEVER FEEL SECURE.

WE'LL KEEP PLAYING PRETEND,
MAKING BELIEVE THAT
WE KNOW WHAT IS REAL.
PLAYING PRETEND,
COVERING UP ALL
THE DOUBTS THAT WE FEEL.
AND OUR LITTLE ACT GOES ON AND ON

MELANIE (CONT)
WITH NO FINISH LINE IN SIGHT,
AND WE YEARN FOR THAT ONE SIMPLE TRUTH,
BUT IT NEVER COMES TO LIGHT.

AND I HATE THAT.

LOGAN
I GET THAT.

LOGAN, MELANIE
IT SUCKS THAT WE'RE STUCK IN A WORLD
THAT'S SHIFTING AND STRANGE.
UNSURE OF HOW TO ACT,
UNSURE OF WHERE WE'RE GOING,
UNSURE OF WHO WE ARE –
AND KNOWING THAT MAY NEVER CHANGE.

LOGAN
THERE FOR EACH OTHER.
WE HAVE TO BE THERE FOR EACH OTHER.
IT'S TRUE THAT THE WORLD MIGHT BE HELL,
OH WELL,
AT LEAST WE WON'T FACE IT ALONE.

MELANIE
THERE FOR EACH OTHER,
FROM NOW ON WE'RE THERE FOR EACH
OTHER.

LOGAN, MELANIE
I MAY NOT BE CERTAIN, BUT THIS IS A SIGN,
WITH YOU BY MY SIDE, I MIGHT BE FINE.

FINE WITH PLAYING PRETEND,
WALKING THROUGH LIFE

LOGAN, MELANIE (CONT)
SIMPLY MAKING BELIEVE.
PLAYING PRETEND,
KNOWING THERE'S MORE
THAN THE THINGS WE PERCEIVE.
THERE ARE VERY FEW THINGS IN THE WORLD
THAT I'M POSITIVE ARE TRUE,
BUT I KNOW I'M NOT PLAYING PRETEND
WHEN I SAY I'M THERE FOR YOU.
I KNOW I'M NOT PLAYING PRETEND
WHEN I SAY I'M FRIENDS WITH YOU.

(They hug)

LOGAN
You know what I think. I think we grab that bus, go back to Lakeshore, and spend spring break sitting in Diversity House, watching stupid movies and eating fro-yo.

(BLOG NOTIFICATION SOUND. LOGAN picks up his phone. The BLOG TRIO APPEARS)

BLOG TRIO
The Gay Card Blog has been deleted.

MELANIE
What is it?

LOGAN
It's nothing. Let's go.

END OF SCENE

SCENE SEVEN

*(LOGAN CROSSES to his laptop, exactly where
he was at the start of the show)*

ALL MEN (EXCEPT LOGAN)
SAY GOODBYE TO THAT TEENAGE BOY,
WHO THOUGHT SOME GUYS HAD NO FEAR.

ALL WOMEN
SAY GOODBYE TO THAT TEENAGE GIRL,
WHO THOUGHT ANSWERS WOULD BE CLEAR.

ALL (EXCEPT LOGAN)
ONE YEAR GONE, THE SUMMER IS WAITING,
WE'RE NEARING MOVE OUT DAY,
AND I THINK BACK ON ALL THE THINGS
I SAID I'D DO BY MAY…

LOGAN
Well, internet, that's my story. So, what do you think? Did I
find myself? Looking at some of these photos from second
semester you'd think so…

HERE'S A PICTURE,
AND IT'S ME THERE,
WITH A WHOLE CROWD BY MY SIDE.
I LOOK HAPPY
AND SO CERTAIN
BUT GUESS WHAT, THE PICTURE LIED.
I WANTED TO GO OUT AND BE LIKE EV'RYBODY

ELSE,
BUT THEN I STARTED LEARNING ABOUT
EV'RYBODY ELSE.
AND THE CRAZY
SCARY TRUTH IS
I'VE BEEN LIKE THEM ALL ALONG.
PAST THE FACES THAT WE SHOW,
PAST THE HANG-UPS THAT WON'T GO,
DON'T WE ALL JUST WANT TO KNOW
WHAT IT FEELS LIKE TO BELONG?

But that's just my experience. What's yours? Leave your
comments down below.

19. AS I GO.. **COMPANY**

(MELANIE STEPS OUT, leaving a comment)

MELANIE
I AM A PERSON WHO WANTS TO BE STRONG,
TO NEED NO ONE ELSE TO BE WHOLE.
BUT THOUGH I MAY KNOW THAT THAT'S
PROBABLY WRONG,
IT'S SCARY TO GIVE UP THAT KIND OF
CONTROL.

(JUSTIN STEPS OUT, leaving a comment)

JUSTIN
I AM A GUY TRYING HARD TO BRANCH OUT,
TO SEE THE UNKNOWN AND DIVE IN.
BUT SOMETIMES IT FEELS, THOUGH YOU FIGHT
EV'RY DOUBT,
YOU CAN'T CATCH A BREAK FROM THE PERSON
YOU'VE BEEN.

MELANIE, JUSTIN
BUT MAYBE, MAYBE,

JUSTIN
THE OLD AND THE NEW YOU
ARE PIECES THAT HAVE TO MELD.

MELANIE, JUSTIN
AND MAYBE, MAYBE,

MELANIE
IT'S TIME TO EASE UP ON
THE PRESSURES YOU'VE ALWAYS HELD.

MELANIE, JUSTIN
GUESS I'LL FIGURE IT OUT AS I GO.

(MELANIE and JUSTIN interact in the real world)

MELANIE
Let me be clear: I want to earn my doctorate by the time I'm twenty-five, I want a real career that won't take a backseat to anyone else's ambitions, I want to revolutionize mathematics with an astounding new discovery – and I want you, terrifying as that sounds.

JUSTIN
I wanna watch football, I wanna drink Bud, I wanna go to gay clubs once a month for the hell of it, and I wanna love you for never judging me for that. Done?

MELANIE
Done.

(They kiss)

DANIELLE
(Commenting on the blog)
I AM A SERIES OF ROLES THAT I PLAY,
A DIVA WHO'S GOT ALL THE STUFF.
BUT STRIP ALL THOSE LAYERS OF COSTUMES
AWAY,
I WORRY THE GIRL
UNDERNEATH'S NOT ENOUGH.

CORY
I AM THESE FEELINGS
THAT CANNOT BE
TAMED,
WITH PASSIONS I PUT
OUT WITH PRIDE.
I SHOUT TO THE WORLD
THAT I DON'T FEEL
ASHAMED,
BUT STILL, THERE ARE
FEARS
THAT I LOCK DEEP
INSIDE.

JULY
I AM A PERSON WHO'S
FOUND PEACE ON
EARTH,
WHO LOOKS TO THE
STARS AS A GUIDE.
I ACT LIKE I'VE GONE
THROUGH REBIRTH,

BUT STILL, THERE ARE
FEARS
THAT I LOCK DEEP
INSIDE.

DANIELLE, CORY, JULY
BUT MAYBE, MAYBE,

CORY, JULY
I'M NOT REALLY LIVING IF I'M NOT FEELING
FEAR.

DANIELLE, CORY, JULY
AND MAYBE, MAYBE,

DANIELLE
THERE'S TRUTH IN THE PLAYING, COULD BE
THE LINE'S NOT CLEAR.

DANIELLE, CORY, JULY
GUESS I'LL FIGURE IT OUT
AS I GO.

(Back to reality)

CORY
So, Logan and Graham really haven't –

JULY
No, but I saw Justin and Melanie holding hands at the library. Guess that's really a thing now.

CORY
I wonder if Danielle –

(DANIELLE ENTERS. THEY go silent)

DANIELLE
Shoulda' locked that down when I had the chance, right?

CORY
You wanna go get drunk and dance it away?

DANIELLE
Nah. Let's stay in. No booze, no dancing, just us.

JULY
I could do a tarot reading!

DANIELLE
That sounds – really good.

LOGAN
(To the audience)
Your responses have been amazing guys. As for those of you
that keep asking about me and Graham… there isn't
anything to tell. I guess sometimes life isn't so great.

MELANIE, JUSTIN, CORY, JULY, DANIELLE
MAYBE, MAYBE,
MAYBE, MAYBE,

(GRAHAM STEPS OUT, commenting)

GRAHAM
I've got a comment for you. My name is Graham Daniels.
And truth be told, I'm the writer of the Gay Card Blog. Talk
about a hypocrite.

I AM A GUY WHO LIED TO YOU ALL
PRETENDED I WAS SOMEONE I'M NOT.

LOGAN
WELL, I MADE A GUY WHO I CARED FOR FEEL
SMALL,
COMPLETELY NEGLECTING
THE FEELINGS HE'S GOT.

LOGAN, GRAHAM
BUT MAYBE, MAYBE,
WE'LL SAY THAT MISTAKES ARE JUST WHAT IT
MEANS TO LIVE.
AND MAYBE, MAYBE,
WE'LL PUT THEM BEHIND US, TRY AGAIN, AND
FORGIVE.
AND WE'LL FIGURE IT OUT
AS WE GO.

(GRAHAM and LOGAN in the real world)

GRAHAM
If I hadn't written that blog –

LOGAN
If I hadn't followed that blog –

GRAHAM
I know you've gotta hate me for what I said –

(LOGAN pulls out a piece of paper)

GRAHAM
What's that?

LOGAN
My Gay Card. The one you made me.

GRAHAM
You kept it?

LOGAN
I mean, I worked awfully hard for it.

(GRAHAM takes the card from him)

GRAHAM
You don't need it anymore.

(He rips it up, and kisses LOGAN)

ENSEMBLE MEN
GUESS WE'LL FIGURE IT OUT

ENSEMBLE WOMEN
WE'LL FIGURE IT OUT

ENSEMBLE
AS WE GO.

LOGAN
(To the audience)
But sometimes, internet, life is awesome!

(GRAHAM, MELANIE, and JUSTIN JOIN LOGAN)

LOGAN
Well, we've got summer break to get to, full of good decisions and bad mistakes. And I plan to embrace every single one – eventually. What do we say guys?

LOGAN, MELANIE, GRAHAM, JUSTIN
Until next time, followers!

ALL
EV'RY STEP'S A STEP ON OUR OWN.
WHERE IT WILL LEAD, I DON'T KNOW.
THOUGH THE ANSWERS HAVEN'T BEEN SHOWN,
THOUGH WE'RE NOT SURE HOW MUCH WE'VE GROWN,

MEN	WOMEN	LOG, GRA, MEL
STARTING NOW…	STARTING NOW…	SAY HELLO TO ANOTHER DAY, WHO CAN
	STARTING NOW…	REALLY SAY
STARTING NOW…		WHAT MIGHT
STARTING NOW…	STARTING NOW…	COME OUR WAY:
		LEARN A TON,
ANSWERS FADE,	I TAKE HEART	FACE A FEAR,
ON WE PLOW,		HAVE SOME
STARTING NOW…	STARTING NOW…	FUN, A CAREER, BUT THE ONE THING THAT'S CLEAR: STARTING NOW…

ALL
WE CAN FIGURE IT OUT
AS WE GO!

(LOGAN closes the laptop. BLACKOUT)

THE END